STUDENT STUDY GUIDE

Geometry

HOLT, RINEHART AND WINSTON

A Harcourt Classroom Education Company

Austin · New York · Orlando · Atlanta · San Francisco · Boston · Dallas · Toronto · London

To the Teacher

Student Study Guide contains one-page reviews for each of the 80 lessons in *Geometry*. Lessons are grouped by chapter and include the following items:

- **Lesson Objectives** contain the objectives listed on the first page of each lesson in the *Pupil's Edition*.
- **Glossary Terms** include boldface terms found in each lesson and defined in the Glossary.
- **Theorems, Postulates, and Definitions** include all boxed theorems, postulates, and definitions.
- **Key Skills** contain a performance-based statement and a related, solved example. This section is taken directly from the Chapter Review section in the *Pupil's Edition*.
- **Exercises** follow the Key Skills sections and provide practice problems similar to the solved example shown in the Key Skills section.

Photo Credit
Front Cover: Dale Sanders/Masterfile.

Printed in the United States of America

ISBN 0-03-054334-7

2   3   4   5   6   7   066   03   02   01

Table of Contents

Student Study Guide

1.1 The Building Blocks of Geometry

Objectives

- Understand and identify the undefined terms *point, line,* and *plane.*
- Define *segment, ray, angle, collinear, intersect, intersection,* and *coplanar.*
- Investigate postulates about points, lines, and planes.

Glossary Terms

angle	collinear	coplanar	exterior of an angle
interior of an angle	intersection	line	plane
point	postulate	ray	
segment	sides of an angle	vertex of an angle	

Theorems, Postulates, and Definitions

Postulate 1.1.4: The intersection of two lines is a point.

Postulate 1.1.5: The intersection of two planes is a line.

Postulate 1.1.6: Through any two points there is one and only one line.

Postulate 1.1.7: Through any three noncollinear points there is one and only one plane.

Postulate 1.1.8: If two points are in a plane, then the line containing them is in the plane.

Key Skills

Identify and name geometric figures.

In the figure, A, B, and C are points, $\overleftrightarrow{AB}$ and $\overleftrightarrow{BC}$ are lines, $\overline{AB}$ and $\overline{BC}$ are segments, $\overrightarrow{BA}$ and $\overrightarrow{BC}$ are rays, and $\angle ABC$ is an angle.

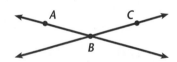

Exercises

1. Name all lines, rays, segments, and angles in the figure.

_____

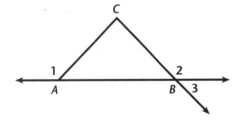

Student Study Guide

1.2 Measuring Length

Objectives

- Construct a geometry ruler.
- Define *length, measure,* and *congruence.*
- Identify and use the Segment Addition Postulate.

Glossary Terms

congruent   coordinates of a point   length   number line

Theorems, Postulates, and Definitions

The Length of $\overline{AB}$: Let A and B be points on a number line, with coordinates a and b. Then the measure of $\overline{AB}$, which is called its length, is $|a - b|$ or $|b - a|$.

Segment Congruence Postulate 1.2.2: If two segments have the same length as measured by a fair ruler, then the segments are congruent. Also, if two segments are congruent, then they have the same length as measured by a fair ruler.

Segment Addition Postulate 1.2.3: If point R is between points P and Q on a line, then $PR + RQ = PQ$.

Key Skills

Determine the length of a given segment.

Find the lengths of $\overline{AB}$, $\overline{BC}$, and $\overline{CD}$.

$AB = |-4 - (-1)| = 3$; $BC = |-1 - 4| = 5$
$CD = |4 - 9| = 5$

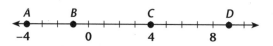

Determine whether segments are congruent.

In the figure above, $\overline{BC} \cong \overline{CD}$, but $\overline{AB}$ is not congruent to the other segments.

Add measures of segments.

$AC = AB + BC = 24 + 40 = 64$

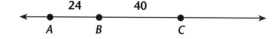

Exercises

1. Find the length of $\overline{DF}$.

_____

2. Point A is between points X and Y on a line. If $XA = 17$ and $AY = 28$, find XY.

_____

3. Point B is between points M and P on a line. If $MP = 54$ and $BP = 15$, find MB.

_____

Student Study Guide

1.3 Measuring Angles

Objectives

- Measure angles with a protractor.
- Identify and use the Angle Addition Postulate.

Glossary Terms

acute angle   complementary angles   linear pair   obtuse angle

right angle   supplementary angles

Theorems, Postulates, and Definitions

Angle Addition Postulate 1.3.2: If point S is in the interior of $\angle PQR$, then $m\angle PQS + m\angle SQR = m\angle PQR$.

Angle Congruence Postulate 1.3.3: If angles have the same measure, then they are congruent. If two angles are congruent, then they have the same measure.

Linear Pair Property: If two angles form a linear pair, then they are supplementary.

Key Skills

Determine the measure of a given angle.

Find the measure of angle $\angle BVC$.

$m\angle BVC = |125° - 50°| = 75°$

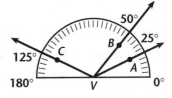

Add measures of angles.

$m\angle AVC = m\angle AVB + m\angle BVC = 25° + 75° = 100°$

Determine whether angles are congruent.

$\angle AVB$ and $\angle BVC$ are not congruent because they do not have the same measure.

Exercises

1. Find $m\angle WVX$ and $m\angle XVY$. _____

2. Find $m\angle WVY$. _____

3. Are $\angle WVX$ and $\angle XVY$ congruent? _____

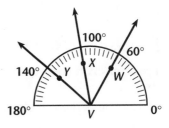

Student Study Guide

1.4 Geometry Using Paper Folding

Objectives

- Use paper folding to construct perpendicular lines, parallel lines, segment bisectors, and angle bisectors.
- Define and make geometry conjectures.

Glossary Terms

angle bisector   conjecture   midpoint   parallel lines
perpendicular bisector   perpendicular lines   segment bisector

Theorems, Postulates, and Definitions

Perpendicular lines are two lines that intersect to form a right angle.

Parallel lines are two coplanar lines that do not intersect.

A *segment bisector* is a line that divides a segment into two congruent parts. The point where a bisector intersects the segment is the *midpoint*.

A *bisector perpendicular* to a segment is called a *perpendicular bisector*.

An *angle bisector* is a line or ray that divides an angle into two congruent angles.

Key Skills

Use paper folding to construct geometric figures.

For the figure at right, construct the perpendicular bisector of $\overline{AB}$, the angle bisector of $\angle ABC$, and a line parallel to $\overleftrightarrow{BC}$ that passes through A.

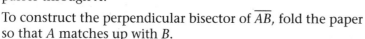

To construct the perpendicular bisector of $\overline{AB}$, fold the paper so that A matches up with B.

To construct the angle bisector of $\angle ABC$, fold the paper so that $\overrightarrow{BA}$ matches up with $\overrightarrow{BC}$.

To construct a line parallel to $\overleftrightarrow{BC}$ that passes through A, fold $\overleftrightarrow{BC}$ onto itself to form a perpendicular. Fold the perpendicular onto itself so that C is on the fold.

Exercises

Trace each figure onto folding paper and construct the given line.

1. a. the perpendicular bisector of $\overline{AB}$
   b. a line parallel to $\overleftrightarrow{AB}$

2. a. the angle bisector of $\angle ABC$
   b. a line perpendicular to $\overleftrightarrow{AB}$ through C

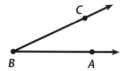

Student Study Guide

1.5 *Special Points in Triangles*

Objectives

- Discover points of concurrency in triangles.
- Draw the inscribed and circumscribed circles of triangles.

Glossary Terms

centroid   circumcenter   circumscribed circle   concurrent

incenter   inscribed circle

Theorems, Postulates, and Definitions

The intersection point of the angles bisectors of the angles of a triangle is the center of the *inscribed* circle of the triangle.

The intersection point of the perpendicular bisectors of the sides of a triangle is the center of the *circumscribed* circle of the triangle.

Key Skills

Find the circumscribed circle of a triangle.

The center of the circumscribed circle of a triangle is the intersection of the perpendicular bisectors of the sides of the triangle.

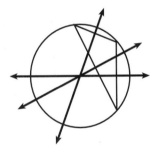

Find the inscribed circle of a triangle.

The center of the inscribed circle of a triangle is the intersection of the angle bisectors of the triangle.

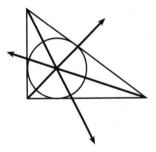

Exercises

Use geometry software or folding paper and a compass to construct the following:

1. Draw a right triangle and construct the perpendicular bisectors of its sides. Where do the perpendicular bisectors meet?

_____

2. Inscribe a circle in an obtuse triangle.

3. Construct a triangle with two congruent sides circumscribed by a circle.

Student Study Guide

1.6 Motion in Geometry

Objective

- Identify the three basic rigid transformations: translation, rotation, and reflection.

Glossary Terms

image   preimage   reflection   rigid transformation
rotation   translation

Theorems, Postulates, and Definitions

Reflection of a Point Across a Line: A point is said to be reflected across a line if and only if the line is the perpendicular bisector of the segment that contains the point and a second point known as the reflected image of the point.

Key Skills

Identify translations, rotations, and reflections.

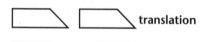

Translate a figure along a line.

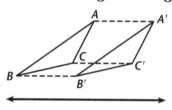

Rotate a figure about a point.

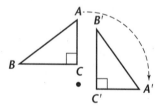

Reflect a figure across a line.

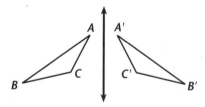

Exercises

1. Translate the figure along the line.

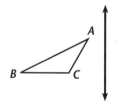

2. Rotate the figure about point P.

3. Reflect the figure across the line.

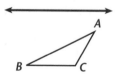

1.7 *Motion in the Coordinate Plane*

Objectives

- Review the algebraic concepts of *coordinate plane, x-* and *y-coordinates,* and *ordered pair.*
- Construct translations, reflections across axes, and rotations about the origin on a coordinate plane.

Theorems, Postulates, and Definitions

Horizontal and Vertical Coordinate Translations

Horizontal translation of *h* units: $H(x, y) = (x + h, y)$
Vertical translation of *v* units: $H(x, y) = (x, y + v)$

Reflections Across the *x-* and *y-*Axes

Reflection across the *x*-axis: $M(x, y) = (x, -y)$
Reflection across the *y*-axis: $N(x, y) = (-x, y)$

180° Rotation About the Origin

$R(x, y) = (-x, -y)$

Key Skills

Use the coordinate plane to transform geometric figures.

To translate 6 units right, use the rule
$H(x, y) = (x + 6, y)$.

To reflect across the *x*-axis, use the rule
$M(x, y) = (x, -y)$.

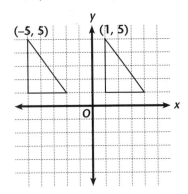

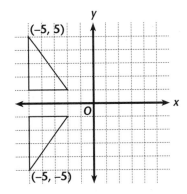

Exercises

A triangle has vertices at (1, 2), (3, 0), and (4, 4). Give the new coordinates of the vertices after each transformation.

1. Translate the triangle 6 units to the left and 2 units down. _____

2. Reflect the triangle across the *y*-axis. _____

3. Rotate the triangle 180° about the origin. _____

Student Study Guide
2.1 An Introduction to Proofs

Objectives

- Investigate some interesting proofs of mathematical claims.
- Understand the meaning of *proof*.

Glossary Terms

formal proof   proof   paragraph proof

Key Skills

Give a paragraph proof of a conjecture.

In the diagram shown the coordinate of A is a and the coordinate of B is b.

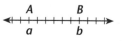

Conjecture: If $b > a$, then the coordinate of the midpoint of $\overline{AB}$ is $\dfrac{a+b}{2}$.

Proof: To find the midpoint $\overline{AB}$, first find half the distance from A to B and then add that distance to a.

Since $b > a$, the distance from a to b is $b - a$. Then half the distance is $\dfrac{b-a}{2}$, or $\dfrac{b}{2} - \dfrac{a}{2}$. Adding half the distance to a in order to find the midpoint

yields $a + \left(\dfrac{b}{2} - \dfrac{a}{2}\right)$, or $a - \dfrac{a}{2} + \dfrac{b}{2}$. Since $a - \dfrac{a}{2} = \dfrac{a}{2}$, the midpoint of $\overline{AB}$ is

$\dfrac{a}{2} + \dfrac{b}{2}$, or $\dfrac{a+b}{2}$.

Exercises

1. How are the terms related in the sequence of numbers being added below?

    $5 + 9 + 13 + 17 + 21 + 25 + 29 + 33 + 37 + 41 + 45 + 49 + 53 + 57 + 61 + 65$

    _____

2. For the sequence in Exercise 1 find the sum of the first number and the last number, the second number and the second-to-last number, and the third number and the third-to-last number. Find the sum of the numbers without adding all of the individual numbers.

    _____

3. Write a paragraph proof of the following conjecture:
    The sum of the first n terms of a sequence formed by repeatedly adding the same number is $\dfrac{n}{2}$(first term + nth term).

    _____

    _____

Student Study Guide

2.2 An Introduction to Logic

Objectives

- Define conditionals and model them with Euler diagrams.
- Use conditionals in logical arguments.
- Form the converses of conditionals.
- Create logical chains from conditionals.

Glossary Terms

conclusion   converse   deductive reasoning   logical chain
conditional   counterexample   hypothesis

Theorems, Postulates, and Definitions

If-Then Transitive Property 2.2.1: Given: "If *A*, then *B*, and if *B*, then *C*." You can conclude: "If *A*, then *C*."

Key Skills

Draw a conclusion from a conditional.

Give the conclusion that follows from these statements:
If a person is in Ms. Robert's 5th period class, then the person is taking geometry.
Claire is in Ms. Robert's 5th period class.

Conclusion: Claire is taking geometry.

State the converse of a conditional.

The converse of the previous conditional is as follows:
If a person is taking geometry, then the person is in Ms. Robert's 5th period class.

Arrange statements in a logical chain and draw a conclusion.

A. If there is no school in Greenfield, Claire will stay home all day.
B. If it snows too much in Greenfield, there is no school in Greenfield.
C. If Claire stays home all day, Claire will go on the Internet.

The order of the statements in the logical chain is **B**, **A**, and **C**.
The conclusion is "If it snows too much in Greenfield, then Claire will go on the Internet."

Exercises

1. What conclusion can be drawn from the following statements? If a person scores 87 on a geometry test, then the person receives a B on the test. Bob scored 87 on the last geometry test.

_____

2. Write the converse of the conditional statement in Exercise 1. Is the converse true?

_____

3. Order the statements below into a logical chain. _____
   A. If it snows, then the roads are slippery.
   B. If it is dangerous to drive, then there will be more accidents than usual.
   C. If the roads are slippery, then it is dangerous to drive.

Student Study Guide
2.3 Definitions

Objectives

- Use Euler diagrams to study definitions of objects.
- Use principles of logic to create definitions of objects.

Glossary Terms

adjacent angles   biconditional

Theorems, Postulates, and Definitions

Definition of Adjacent Angles: Adjacent angles are angles in a plane
that have their vertices and one side in common but that do not overlap.

Key Skills

Write a definition of an object.

These objects are rhombuses.   These objects are not rhombuses.

Which of the following objects are rhombuses? Write a definition of a rhombus.

a.   b.   c.   d.

Objects **a** and **d** are rhombuses. A rhombus is a four-sided figure in which
all four sides have the same length.

Determine whether a statement is a definition.

Is the following statement a definition? "The sum of the angles that form a linear pair
is 180°."
If a statement is a definition, then the conditional form and its converse are both true.

Conditional: If two angles form a linear pair, then the sum of their angles is 180°.
Converse: If the sum of two angles is 180°, then the angles form a linear pair.

Since the converse is false, the statement is not a definition.

Exercises

These objects are kites.   These objects are not kites.

1. Which of these objects are kites? _____   **2.** Write a definition of a kite.

a. b. c. d.

_____

_____

3. Is the statement below a definition? Why or why not? _____
     Two parallel lines do not intersect.

Student Study Guide

2.4 Building a System of Geometry Knowledge

Objectives

- Identify and use the Algebraic Properties of Equality.
- Identify and use the Equivalence Properties of Equality and of Congruence.
- Link the steps of a proof by using properties and postulates.

Glossary Terms

Addition Property   Reflexive Property   Subtraction Property   theorem
Division Property   Substitution Property   Symmetric Property   Transitive Property
Multiplication Property

Theorems, Postulates, and Definitions

Overlapping Segments Theorem 2.4.6: Given a segment with points
A, B, C, and D arranged as shown, the following statements are true:

1. If $AB = CD$, then $AC = BD$.
2. If $AC = BD$, then $AB = CD$.

Overlapping Angles Theorem 2.4.13: Given $\angle AVD$ with points B and
C in its interior as shown, the following statements are true:

1. If $m\angle AVB = m\angle CVD$, then $m\angle AVC = m\angle BVD$.
2. If $m\angle AVC = m\angle BVD$, then $m\angle AVB = m\angle CVD$.

Key Skills

Use the Properties of Equality and Congruence to write proofs.

In the figure shown, $m\angle 1 + m\angle 3 = 180°$. Prove that $m\angle 3 = m\angle 2$.

Statements	Reasons
$m\angle 1 + m\angle 3 = 180°$	Given
$m\angle 1 + m\angle 2 = 180°$	Linear Pair Property
$m\angle 1 + m\angle 3 = m\angle 1 + m\angle 2$	Substitution Property
$m\angle 3 = m\angle 2$	Subtraction Property

Exercises

1. In the figure shown, $m\angle 2 + m\angle 3 + m\angle 4 = 180°$.
Prove that $m\angle 1 = m\angle 3 + m\angle 4$.

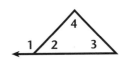

_____

_____

_____

_____

_____

_____

Student Study Guide

2.5 Conjectures That Lead to Theorems

Objectives

- Develop theorems from conjectures.
- Write two-column and paragraph proofs.

Glossary Terms

inductive reasoning   paragraph proof   two-column proof   vertical angles

Theorems, Postulates, and Definitions

Vertical Angles Theorem 2.5.1: If two angles form a pair of vertical angles, then they are congruent.

Theorem 2.5.2: Reflection across two parallel lines is equivalent to a translation of twice the distance between the lines and in a direction perpendicular to the lines.

Theorem 2.5.3: Reflection across two intersecting lines is equivalent to a rotation about the point of intersection through twice the measure of the angle between the lines.

Key Skills

Use deductive reasoning to prove a conjecture.

Given: In the figure shown, m∠1 + m∠3 = m∠2 + m∠3.
Prove: m∠4 = m∠5

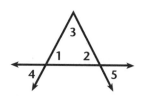

Statements	Reasons
m∠1 + m∠3 = m∠2 + m∠3	Given
m∠1 = m∠2	Subtraction Property
m∠1 = m∠4 ; m∠2 = m∠5	Vertical Angles Theorem
m∠4 = m∠5	Substitution Property

Exercises

1. Given: In the figure shown, m∠1 + m∠2 = 180°.
Prove: m∠3 = m∠4

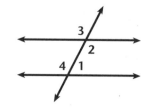

_____

_____

_____

_____

_____

_____

_____

 **Student Study Guide**

3.1 *Symmetry in Polygons*

Objectives

- Define *polygon.*
- Define and use *reflectional symmetry* and *rotational symmetry.*
- Define *regular polygon, center of a regular polygon, central angle of a regular polygon,* and *axis of symmetry.*

Glossary Terms

axis of symmetry	center point	central angle	equiangular polygon
equilateral polygon	polygon	reflectional symmetry	regular polygon
rotational symmetry	sides of a polygon	vertices of a polygon	

Theorems, Postulates, and Definitions

Triangles Classified by Number of Congruent Sides

Three congruent sides:	equilateral
At least two congruent sides:	isosceles
No congruent sides:	scalene

Reflectional Symmetry

A figure has reflectional symmetry if and only if its reflected image across a line coincides with the preimage. The line is called an *axis of symmetry.*

Rotational Symmetry

A figure has rotational symmetry if and only if it has at least one rotation image, not counting rotation images of 0° or multiples of 360°, that coincides with the original image.

Key Skills

Identify reflectional symmetry of figures.

Draw all axes of symmetry for the figure at right.

Identify rotational symmetry of figures.

Describe the rotational symmetry of the figure at right.

The figure has 4-fold rotational symmetry. The image will coincide with the original figure after rotations of 90°, 180°, 270°, and 360°. At 360°, the figure is returned to its original position.

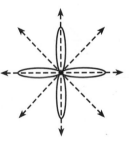

Exercises

Draw all axes of symmetry and describe the rotational symmetry of each figure.

1. _____

2. _____

Student Study Guide

3.2 Properties of Quadrilaterals

Objectives

- Define *quadrilateral, parallelogram, rhombus, rectangle, square,* and *trapezoid.*
- Identify the properties of quadrilaterals and the relationships among the properties.

Glossary Terms

parallelogram   quadrilateral   rectangle   rhombus
square   trapezoid

Key Skills

Make conjectures about the properties of quadrilaterals.

In a *parallelogram,* the opposite sides and angles are congruent, the diagonals bisect each other, and consecutive angles are supplementary.

In a *rhombus,* the diagonals are perpendicular to each other.

In a *rectangle,* the diagonals are congruent.

In a *trapezoid,* if the two sides that are not parallel are congruent, then the diagonals are congruent.

A *square* is a parallelogram, a rectangle, and a rhombus.

Exercises

1. *ABCD* is a parallelogram with m∠*ADC* = 45°. Find m∠1 and m∠2.

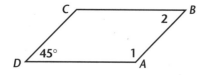

2. *ABCD* is a parallelogram with *DO* = 10 meters and *AB* = 8 meters. Find *OB* and *CD*.

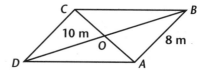

_____

3. *ABCD* is a rectangle with *AO* = 6 inches. Find m∠*BCD* and *BD*.

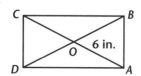

4. *ABCD* is a rhombus with m∠*ADC* = 125°. Find m∠1 and m∠*BCD*.

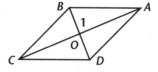

_____

Student Study Guide

3.3 Parallel Lines and Transversals

Objectives

- Define *transversal, alternate interior angles, alternate exterior angles, same-side interior angles,* and *corresponding angles.*
- Make conjectures and prove theorems by using postulates and properties of parallel lines and transversals.

Glossary Terms

alternate exterior angles
same-side interior angles

alternate interior angles
transversal

corresponding angles

Theorems, Postulates, and Definitions

Corresponding Angles Postulate 3.3.2: If two lines cut by a transversal are parallel, then corresponding angles are congruent.

Alternate Interior Angles Theorem 3.3.3: If two lines cut by a transversal are parallel, then alternate interior angles are congruent.

Alternate Exterior Angles Theorem 3.3.4: If two lines cut by a transversal are parallel, then alternate exterior angles are congruent.

Same-Side Interior Angles Theorem 3.3.5: If two lines cut by a transversal are parallel, then same-side interior angles are supplementary.

Key Skills

Identify special angle pairs.

In the diagram shown, $\angle 1$ and $\angle 5$ are corresponding angles, $\angle 1$ and $\angle 3$ are alternate interior angles, $\angle 1$ and $\angle 4$ are same-side interior angles, and $\angle 2$ and $\angle 5$ are alternate exterior angles.

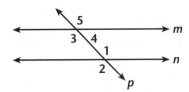

Find angle measures formed by parallel lines and transversals.

In the diagram shown, $m \parallel n$ and $m\angle 1 = 135°$, so $m\angle 2 = m\angle 3 = m\angle 5 = 135°$ and $m\angle 4 = 45°$.

Exercises

1. a. Which of the numbered angles are corresponding angles?

_____

b. Which of the numbered angles are same-side interior angles?

_____

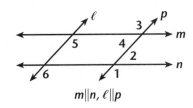

$m \parallel n, \ell \parallel p$

2. If $m\angle 1 = 120°$ in the diagram above, find $m\angle 3$, $m\angle 4$, and $m\angle 6$. _____

3. In the diagram above, find $m\angle 4$ if $m\angle 4 = (2x - 20)°$ and $m\angle 5 = (3x + 10)°$. _____

Student Study Guide

3.4 Proving That Lines Are Parallel

Objectives

- Identify and use the converse of the Corresponding Angles Postulate.
- Prove that lines are parallel by using theorems and postulates.

Theorems, Postulates, and Definitions

Theorem: Converse of the Corresponding Angles Postulate 3.4.1:
If two lines are cut by a transversal in such a way that corresponding angles are congruent, then the two lines are parallel.

Converse of the Same-Side Interior Angles Theorem 3.4.2: If two lines are cut by a transversal in such a way that same-side interior angles are supplementary, then the two lines are parallel.

Converse of the Alternate Interior Angles Theorem 3.4.3: If two lines are cut by a transversal in such a way that alternate interior angles are congruent, then the two lines are parallel.

Converse of the Alternate Exterior Angles Theorem 3.4.4: If two lines are cut by a transversal in such a way that alternate exterior angles are congruent, then the two lines are parallel.

Theorem 3.4.5: If two coplanar lines are perpendicular to the same line, then the two lines are parallel.

Theorem 3.4.6: If two coplanar lines are parallel to the same line, then the two lines are parallel.

Key Skills

Use the converses of the transversal theorems and postulates to prove that lines are parallel.

Given: the diagram at right with $m\angle 1 + m\angle 3 = 180°$
Prove: Lines m and line n are parallel.

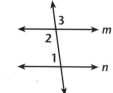

Statements	Reasons
$m\angle 1 + m\angle 3 = 180°$	Given
$m\angle 2 = m\angle 3$	Vertical Angles Theorem
$m\angle 1 + m\angle 2 = 180°$	Substitution Property
$m \parallel n$	Converse of the Same-Side Interior Angles Theorem

Exercises

1. Given: $m\angle 1 + m\angle 3 = 180°$
Prove: $m \parallel n$

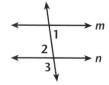

_____

_____

_____

_____

Student Study Guide

3.5 The Triangle Sum Theorem

Objective

- Identify and use the Parallel Postulate and the Triangle Sum Theorem.

Glossary Terms

exterior angle   remote interior angle

Theorems, Postulates, and Definitions

The Parallel Postulate 3.5.1: Given a line and a point not on the line, there is one and only one line that contains the given point and is parallel to the given line.

Triangle Sum Theorem 3.5.2: The sum of the measures of the angles of a triangle is 180°.

Exterior Angle Theorem 3.5.3: The measure of an exterior angle of a triangle is equal to the sum of the measures of the remote interior angles.

Key Skills

Use the Triangle Sum Theorem to find angle measures.

Find the measure of ∠2.

By the Vertical Angles Theorem, m∠1 = 57°.
By the Triangle Sum Theorem, m∠2 + 57° + 70° = 180°.
Thus, m∠ 2 = 180° − 70° − 57° = 53°.

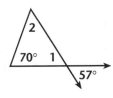

Exercises

1. Find m∠1. _____

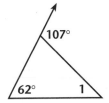

2. Find m∠1. _____

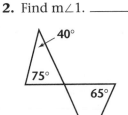

3. If $m \parallel n$, find m∠1 and m∠2.

_____

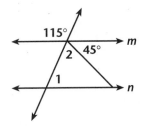

4. Find m∠1 if m∠1 = $(3x + 5)°$, m∠2 = $(2x + 10)°$, and m∠3 = $(5x − 25)°$.

_____

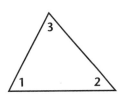

Student Study Guide

3.6 Angles in Polygons

Objectives

- Define interior and exterior angles of a polygon.
- Develop and use formulas for the sums of the measures of interior and exterior angles of a polygon.

Glossary Terms

concave polygon   convex polygon

Theorems, Postulates, and Definitions

Sum of the Interior Angles of a Polygon 3.6.1: The sum, s, of the measures of the interior angles of a polygon with n sides is given by $s = (n - 2)180°$.

The Measure of an Interior Angle of a Regular Polygon 3.6.2:
The measure, m, of an interior angle of a regular polygon with n sides is given by $m = 180° - \dfrac{360°}{n}$.

Sum of the Exterior Angles of a Polygon 3.6.3: The sum of the measures of the exterior angles of a polygon is 360°.

Key Skills

Find interior and exterior angle measures in polygons.

Find the sum of the measures of the interior angles and of the exterior angles of a polygon with 15 sides.

The sum of the measures of the interior angles is $(15 - 2)180° = 2340°$.

The measure of each interior angle of a regular polygon with 15 sides is
$180° - \dfrac{360°}{15} = 156°$.

The sum of the measures of the exterior angles is 360°.

Exercises

1. Find the sum of the interior angles of a polygon with 18 sides. _____

2. Find the measure of each interior angle of a regular polygon with 24 sides. _____

3. If each exterior angle of a regular polygon has a measure of 12°, how many sides does the polygon have? _____

4. In the pentagon below, $m\angle 1 = (5x - 5)°$, $m\angle 2 = (4x + 15)°$, and $m\angle 3 = (8x - 10)°$. Find $m\angle 1$.

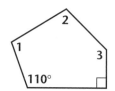

5. Find x in the hexagon below.

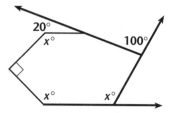

Student Study Guide

3.7 Midsegments of Triangles and Trapezoids

Objectives

- Define *midsegment of a triangle* and *midsegment of a trapezoid*.
- Develop and use formulas from the properties of triangle and trapezoid midsegments.

Glossary Terms

midsegment of a trapezoid   midsegment of a triangle

Theorems, Postulates, and Definitions

Midsegment of a Triangle: A midsegment of a triangle is a segment whose endpoints are the midpoints of two sides.

Midsegment of a Trapezoid: A midsegment of a trapezoid is a segment whose endpoints are the midpoints of the nonparallel sides.

Key Skills

Solve problems by using triangle and trapezoid midsegments.

In the diagram shown, $\overline{DE}$ is a midsegment of $\triangle ABC$, $\overline{FG}$ is a midsegment of trapezoid $ABED$, and $AB = 80$ meters. Find DE and FG.

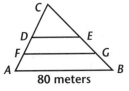

The length of a midsegment of a triangle is half the length of the base, so $DE = \dfrac{80}{2} = 40$ meters.

The length of a midsegment of a trapezoid is the average of the lengths of the bases, so $FG = \dfrac{80 + 40}{2} = 60$ meters.

Exercises

1. The length of one side of a triangle is 46 meters. Find the length of the midsegment that connects the other two sides of the triangle.

_____

2. The length of one base of a trapezoid is 45 centimeters and the length of the midsegment of the trapezoid is 62 centimeters. Find the length of the other base of the trapezoid.

_____

3. In the diagram below, $\overline{DE}$ is a midsegment of $\triangle ABC$. Find $m\angle 1$ and AB.

4. In the diagram below, $\overline{EF}$ is a midsegment of trapezoid $ABCD$. Find EF.

# Student Study Guide
3.8 Analyzing Polygons Using Coordinates

Objectives ⁓⁓

- Develop and use theorems about equal slopes and slopes of perpendicular lines.
- Solve problems involving perpendicular and parallel lines in the coordinate plane by using appropriate theorems.

Glossary Terms ⁓⁓

hypotenuse   rise   run   slope

Theorems, Postulates, and Definitions ⁓⁓

Slope Formula: The slope of a nonvertical line that contains the points (x_1, y_1) and (x_2, y_2) is the following ratio: $\dfrac{y_2 - y_1}{x_2 - x_1}$.

Parallel Lines Theorem 3.8.2: Two nonvertical lines are parallel if and only if they have the same slope. Any two vertical lines are parallel.

Perpendicular Lines Theorem 3.8.3: Two nonvertical lines are perpendicular if and only if the product of their slopes is -1. Any vertical line is perpendicular to any horizontal line.

Midpoint Formula: The midpoint of a segment with endpoints (x_1, y_1) and (x_2, y_2) has coordinates $\left(\dfrac{x_1 + x_2}{2}, \dfrac{y_1 + y_2}{2}\right)$.

Key Skills ⁓⁓

Use slope to determine whether lines and segments are parallel or perpendicular.

A quadrilateral has vertices $A(2, 3)$, $B(6, 4)$, $C(8, 7)$, and $D(4, 6)$. Is $ABCD$ a parallelogram?

The slope of $\overline{AB}$ is $\dfrac{1}{4}$, the slope of $\overline{BC}$ is $\dfrac{3}{2}$, the slope of $\overline{CD}$ is $\dfrac{1}{4}$, and the slope of $\overline{DA}$ is $\dfrac{3}{2}$.

$\overline{AB}$ and $\overline{CD}$ have the same slope, so they are parallel. $\overline{BC}$ and $\overline{DA}$ are also parallel. Since the opposite sides of quadrilateral $ABCD$ are parallel, $ABCD$ is a parallelogram.

Exercises ⁓⁓

1. Is the segment with endpoints $(3, 7)$ and $(5, 2)$ parallel or perpendicular to the segment with endpoints $(-2, 4)$ and $(-7, 2)$? _____

2. Is the segment with endpoints $(-9, 1)$ and $(3, 4)$ parallel or perpendicular to the segment with endpoints $(6, 2)$ and $(-10, -2)$? _____

3. Find the midpoint of the segment with endpoints $(5, 9)$ and $(-9, 13)$. _____

4. One endpoint of a segment is $(6, -4)$ and the midpoint of the segment is $(-3, 1)$. Find the other endpoint of the segment. _____

Student Study Guide

4.1 Congruent Polygons

Objectives

- Define *congruent polygons*.
- Solve problems by using congruent polygons.

Glossary Terms

congruent polygons   corresponding angles   corresponding sides

Theorems, Postulates, and Definitions

Polygon Congruence Postulate 4.1.1: Two polygons are congruent if and only if there is a correspondence between their sides and angles so that

1. all pairs of corresponding angles are congruent.

2. all pairs of corresponding sides are congruent.

Key Skills

Identify corresponding parts of congruent polygons.

Given quadrilateral $ABCD \cong$ quadrilateral $WXYZ$, identify all pairs of congruent sides and angles.

$\overline{AB} \cong \overline{WX}, \overline{BC} \cong \overline{XY}, \overline{CD} \cong \overline{YZ}, \overline{DA} \cong \overline{ZW}$,
$\angle A \cong \angle W, \angle B \cong \angle X, \angle C \cong \angle Y, \angle D \cong \angle Z$

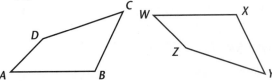

Exercises

In the diagram shown, pentagon $ABCDE \cong$ pentagon $VWXYZ$. Complete the following congruence statements:

1. $\overline{CD} \cong$ _____

2. $\overline{ZV} \cong$ _____

3. $\angle Y \cong$ _____

4. $\angle EAB \cong$ _____

5. pentagon $DCBAE \cong$ _____

6. Given hexagon $ABCDEF \cong$ hexagon $TUVWXY$, write three congruence statements.

_____

Student Study Guide

4.2 Triangle Congruence

Objectives

- Explore triangle rigidity.
- Develop three congruence postulates for triangles—SSS, SAS, and ASA.

Glossary Terms

included angle   included side   triangle rigidity

Theorems, Postulates, and Definitions

SSS (Side-Side-Side) Postulate 4.2.1: If the sides of one triangle are congruent to the sides of another triangle, then the two triangles are congruent.

SAS (Side-Angle-Side) Postulate 4.2.2: If two sides and the included angle in one triangle are congruent to two sides and the included angle in another triangle, then the two triangles are congruent.

ASA (Angle-Side-Angle) Postulate 4.2.3: If two angles and the included side in one triangle are congruent to two angles and the included side in another triangle, then the two triangles are congruent.

Key Skills

Use SSS, SAS, and ASA postulates to determine whether triangles are congruent.

Name the postulate that allows you to conclude the following:

a. $\triangle ABC \cong \triangle ADC$ (SSS Postulate)

b. $\triangle PRS \cong \triangle XYZ$ (SAS Postulate)

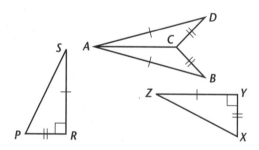

Exercises

Identify the congruent triangles and name the postulate that supports your answer.

1. _____

2. _____

3. _____

4. _____

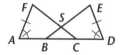

Student Study Guide

4.3 *Analyzing Triangle Congruence*

Objectives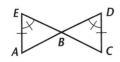

- Identify and use the SSS, SAS, and ASA Congruence Postulates and the AAS and HL Congruence Theorems.
- Use counterexamples to prove that other side and angle combinations cannot be used to prove triangle congruence.

Theorems, Postulates, and Definitions

AAS (Angle-Angle-Side) Congruence Theorem 4.3.1: If two angles and a nonincluded side of one triangle are congruent to the corresponding angles and nonincluded side of another triangle, then the two triangles are congruent.

HL (Hypotenuse-Leg) Congruence Theorem 4.3.2: If the hypotenuse and a leg of one right triangle are congruent to the hypotenuse and corresponding leg of another right triangle, then the two triangles are congruent.

Key Skills

Use AAS and HL Theorems to determine whether triangles are congruent. Identify angle-side combinations that do not establish triangle congruence.

Name the theorem that allows you to conclude that the triangles are congruent. If the triangles are not congruent, state why.

a. $\triangle ABC \cong \triangle DCB$ by HL
b. $\triangle WXY \cong \triangle WZY$ by AAS
c. $\triangle PRS$ might not be congruent to $\triangle ONM$ because triangles cannot be proven congruent by SSA.

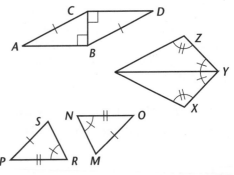

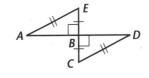

Exercises

Identify the congruent triangles and name the postulate that supports your answer. If the triangles are not congruent, state why.

1. _____

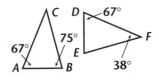

2. _____

3. _____

4. _____

Student Study Guide
4.4 Using Triangle Congruence

Objectives

- Use congruence of triangles to claim congruence of corresponding parts.
- Develop and use the Isosceles Triangle Theorem.

Glossary Terms

base angle   CPCTC   legs   vertex angle

Theorems, Postulates, and Definitions

Isosceles Triangle Theorem 4.4.1: If two sides of a triangle are congruent, then the angles opposite those sides are congruent.

Converse of the Isosceles Triangle Theorem 4.4.2: If two angles of a triangle are congruent, then the sides opposite those angles are congruent.

Corollary 4.4.3: The measure of each angle of an equilateral triangle is 60°.

Corollary 4.4.4: The bisector of the vertex angle of an isosceles triangle is the perpendicular bisector of the base.

Key Skills

Use triangle congruence in proofs.

Given: the diagram at right with $\overline{AC} \cong \overline{CD}$ and $\overline{BC} \cong \overline{EC}$
Prove: $\overline{AB} \cong \overline{DE}$

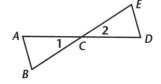

Statements	Reasons
$\overline{AC} \cong \overline{CD}$ and $\overline{BC} \cong \overline{EC}$	Given
$\angle 1 \cong \angle 2$	Vertical Angles Theorem
$\triangle ABC \cong \triangle DEC$	SAS Theorem
$\overline{AB} \cong \overline{DE}$	CPCTC

Use properties of isosceles triangles in proofs.

Given: the diagram at right with $\overline{DC} \cong \overline{EC}$ and $\overline{AB} \parallel \overline{DE}$
Prove: $\overline{AC} \cong \overline{BC}$

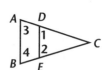

Statements	Reasons
$\overline{DC} \cong \overline{EC}$ and $\overline{AB} \parallel \overline{DE}$	Given
$\angle 1 \cong \angle 2$	Isosceles Triangle Theorem
$\angle 1 \cong \angle 3$ and $\angle 2 \cong \angle 4$	Corresponding Angles Postulate
$\angle 3 \cong \angle 4$	Substitution Property
$\overline{AC} \cong \overline{BC}$	Converse of the Isosceles Triangle Theorem

Exercises

1. Given: $\overline{AB} \cong \overline{DC}$, $\overline{AF} \cong \overline{DE}$, and $n \parallel m$
Prove: $\overline{BE} \cong \overline{CF}$

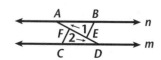

_____

_____

_____

4.5 Proving Quadrilateral Properties

Objective

- Prove quadrilateral conjectures by using triangle congruence postulates and theorems.

Theorems, Postulates, and Definitions

Theorem 4.5.1: A diagonal of a parallelogram divides the parallelogram into two congruent triangles.

Corollary 4.5.2: The opposite sides of a parallelogram are congruent.

Corollary 4.5.3: The opposite angles of a parallelogram are congruent.

Theorem 4.5.4: The diagonals of a parallelogram bisect each other.

Theorem 4.5.5: A rhombus is a parallelogram.

Theorem 4.5.6: A rectangle is a parallelogram.

Theorem 4.5.7: The diagonals and sides of a rhombus form four congruent triangles.

Theorem 4.5.8: The diagonals of a rhombus are perpendicular.

Theorem 4.5.9: The diagonals of a rectangle are congruent.

Theorem 4.5.10: The diagonals of a kite are perpendicular.

Theorem 4.5.11: A square is a rectangle.

Theorem 4.5.12: A square is a rhombus.

Theorem 4.5.13: The diagonals of a square are congruent and are the perpendicular bisectors of each other.

Key Skills

Prove properties of quadrilaterals.

Given: Rhombus $ABCD$
Prove: $\angle 1 \cong \angle 2 \cong \angle 3 \cong \angle 4$

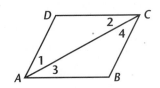

Because a rhombus is a parallelogram and a diagonal of a parallelogram divides the parallelogram into two congruent triangles, $\triangle ABC \cong \triangle CDA$. By CPCTC, $\angle 1 \cong \angle 4$ and $\angle 2 \cong \angle 3$. By definition of a rhombus, $\overline{AB} \cong \overline{BC} \cong \overline{CD} \cong \overline{DA}$, so $\triangle ABC$ and $\triangle CDA$ are isosceles triangles. By the Isosceles Triangle Theorem, $\angle 1 \cong \angle 2$ and $\angle 3 \cong \angle 4$. Using the Substitution Property, $\angle 1 \cong \angle 2 \cong \angle 3 \cong \angle 4$.

Exercises

1. Given: $ABCD$ is a parallelogram and $\overline{AF} \cong \overline{CE}$.
   Prove: $\triangle AFD \cong \triangle CEB$

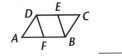

2. Given: $ABCD$ is a rectangle.
   Prove: $\angle 1 \cong \angle 2$

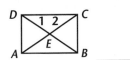

Student Study Guide

4.6 Conditions for Special Quadrilaterals

Objective

- Develop conjectures about special quadrilaterals—parallelograms, rectangles, and rhombuses.

Theorems, Postulates, and Definitions

Theorem 4.6.1: If two pairs of opposite sides of a quadrilateral are congruent, then the quadrilateral is a parallelogram.

Theorem 4.6.2: If one pair of opposite sides of a quadrilateral are parallel and congruent, then the quadrilateral is a parallelogram.

Theorem 4.6.3: If the diagonals of a quadrilateral bisect each other, then the quadrilateral is a parallelogram.

Theorem 4.6.4: If one angle of a parallelogram is a right angle, then the parallelogram is a rectangle.

The Homebuilder Theorem 4.6.5: If the diagonals of a parallelogram are congruent, then the parallelogram is a rectangle.

Theorem 4.6.6: If one pair of adjacent sides of a parallelogram are congruent, then the parallelogram is a rhombus.

Theorem 4.6.7: If the diagonals of a parallelogram bisect the angles of the parallelogram, then the parallelogram is a rhombus.

Theorem 4.6.8: If the diagonals of a parallelogram are perpendicular, then the parallelogram is a rhombus.

The Triangle Midsegment Theorem 4.6.9: A midsegment of a triangle is parallel to a side of the triangle, and its length is half the length of that side.

Key Skills

Classify quadrilaterals from given information.

Is quadrilateral *ABCD* a parallelogram?

Because the diagonals of *ABCD* bisect each other, *ABCD* is a parallelogram.

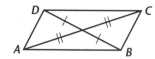

Exercises

Classify each quadrilateral. List all terms that apply to each quadrilateral.

1. _____

2. _____

3. _____

$\overline{AB} \parallel \overline{CD}$

4. _____

Student Study Guide

4.7 Compass and Straightedge Constructions

Objectives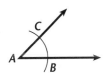

- Construct congruent copies of segments, angles, and triangles.
- Construct an angle bisector.

Key Skills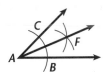

Construct figures by using a compass and straightedge.

Given $\angle A$ below, construct its bisector.

Follow steps **a–b** to construct the bisector of $\angle A$.

a. Place your compass point at A and draw an arc through the rays of the angle. Label the intersection points B and C.

b. Place your compass point first at B and then at C. Use the same compass setting to draw arcs that intersect the interior of $\angle A$. Label the intersection F. Draw a ray from A through F. $\overrightarrow{AF}$ is the bisector of $\angle BAC$.

Exercises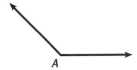

Complete each construction.

1. Construct the perpendicular bisector of $\overline{AB}$.

2. Construct a line through A perpendicular to line m.

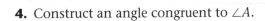

3. Construct the bisector of $\angle A$.

4. Construct an angle congruent to $\angle A$.

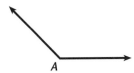

Student Study Guide

4.8 Constructing Transformations

Objectives

- Translate, rotate, and reflect figures by using a compass and straightedge.
- Prove that translations, rotations, and reflections preserve congruence and other properties.
- Use the Betweenness Postulate to establish the Triangle Inequality Theorem.

Glossary Terms

betweenness   isometries

Theorems, Postulates, and Definitions

Betweenness Postulate 4.8.1: Given three points P, Q, and R, if $PQ + QR = PR$, then P, Q, and R are collinear and Q is between P and R.

Triangle Inequality Theorem 4.8.2: The sum of the lengths of any two sides of a triangle is greater than the length of the third side.

Key Skills

Construct translations, rotations, and reflections by using a compass and straightedge.

Translate $\overline{AB}$ by the direction and distance of the given translation vector.

Extend the line that contains $\overline{AB}$ so that it intersects the line that contains the translation vector. Construct line m through point A parallel to the translation vector. Construct line n through point B parallel to the translation vector. Set your compass to the length, s, of the translation vector. On the right side of $\overline{AB}$, construct points A' and B' that are a distance s from points A and B on lines m and n, respectively. Connect points A' and B', so $\overline{AB} \cong \overline{A'B'}$.

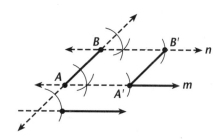

Exercises

1. Reflect $\overline{AB}$ across line m.

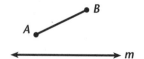

2. If two sides of a triangle have lengths of 12 meters and 20 meters, what are the possible lengths of the third side of the triangle?

Student Study Guide

5.1 Perimeter and Area

Objectives

- Identify and use the Area of a Rectangle Postulate and the Sum of Areas Postulate.
- Solve problems involving fixed perimeters and fixed areas.

Glossary Terms

area   circumference   nonoverlapping   perimeter

Theorems, Postulates, and Definitions

Postulate: The Sum of Areas 5.1.3: If a figure is composed of nonoverlapping regions A and B, then the area of the figure is the sum of the areas of regions A and B.

Postulate: Area of a Rectangle 5.1.4: The area of a rectangle with base b and height h is $A = bh$.

The Perimeter of a Rectangle 5.1.5: The perimeter of a rectangle with base b and height h is $P = 2b + 2h$.

Key Skills

Find the perimeter of a polygon.

Find the perimeter of the polygon at right.

The perimeter of the polygon is $15 + 5 + 7 + 9 + 16 + 7 = 59$ inches.

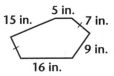

Find the area of a rectangle.

Find the area of the rectangle at right.

The base of the rectangle is 15 meters and the height of the rectangle is 8 meters, so the area is $8 \times 15 = 120$ square meters.

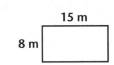

Exercises

1. Find the perimeter of this polygon.

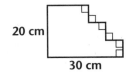

2. Find the area and perimeter of this rectangle.

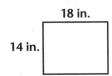

Student Study Guide

5.2 Areas of Triangles, Parallelograms, and Trapezoids

Objectives ～～

- Develop formulas for the areas of triangles, parallelograms, and trapezoids.
- Solve problems by using the formulas for the areas of triangles, parallelograms, and trapezoids.

Glossary Terms ～～

altitude of a parallelogram
base of a parallelogram
height of a parallelogram
kite

altitude of a trapezoid
base of a triangle
height of a trapezoid
legs of a trapezoid

altitude of a triangle
bases of a trapezoid
height of a triangle
midsegment of a trapezoid

Theorems, Postulates, and Definitions ～～

Area of a Triangle: For a triangle with base b and height h, the area, A, is given by $A = \frac{1}{2}bh$.

Area of a Parallelogram: For a parallelogram with base b and height h, the area, A, is given by $A = bh$.

Area of a Trapezoid: For a trapezoid with bases b_1 and b_2 and height h, the area, A, is given by $A = \frac{1}{2}(b_1 + b_2)h$.

Key Skills ～～

Find the area of a triangle.

Find the area of $\triangle ABD$.

The area of $\triangle ABD$ is $\frac{1}{2}(18)(7) = 63$ square meters.

Find the area of a parallelogram.

Find the area of parallelogram $MNOP$.

The area of $MNOP$ is $(16)(9) = 144$ square feet.

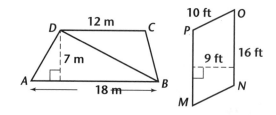

Find the area of a trapezoid.

Find the area of trapezoid $ABCD$.

The area of $ABCD$ is $\frac{1}{2}(18 + 12)(7) = 105$ square meters.

Exercises ～～

1. Find the area of $\triangle ABD$ and parallelogram $ABCD$.

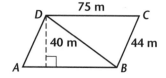

2. Find the area of $\triangle BCD$ and trapezoid $ABDF$.

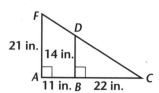

Student Study Guide

5.3 *Circumferences and Areas of Circles*

Objectives

- Identify and apply formulas for the circumference and area of a circle.
- Solve problems by using the formulas for the circumference and area of a circle.

Glossary Terms

circle   diameter   radius   sector

Theorems, Postulates, and Definitions

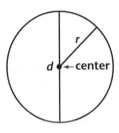

Circle: A circle is the set of all points on a plane that are the same distance r from a given point in the plane known as the center of the circle. The distance r is known as the radius of a circle. The distance $d = 2r$ is known as the diameter of a circle.

Circumference of a Circle 5.3.2: The circumference, C, of a circle with diameter d and radius r is $C = \pi d = 2\pi r$.

Area of a Circle 5.3.3: The area of a circle with radius r is $A = \pi r^2$.

Key Skills

Find the circumference of a circle.

Find the circumference of a circle with a radius of 10 inches.

$C = (2)(\pi)(10) = 20\pi \approx 62.83$ inches

Find the area of a circle.

Find the area of a circle with a radius of 8 meters.

$A = (\pi)(8^2) = 64\pi \approx 201.06$ square meters

Exercises

1. Find the circumference and area of a circle with a radius of 15 feet. _____

2. Find the circumference and area of a circle with a diameter of 26 meters. _____

3. Find the area of a circle with a circumference of 12π inches. _____

4. Find the area of the shaded region in the figure below. _____

12 m

12 m

Student Study Guide

5.4 *The Pythagorean Theorem*

Objectives

- Identify and apply the Pythagorean Theorem and its converse.
- Solve problems by using the Pythagorean Theorem.

Glossary Terms

hypotenuse   Pythagorean triple

Theorems, Postulates, and Definitions

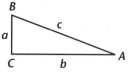

Pythagorean Theorem 5.4.1: For any right triangle, the square of the length of the hypotenuse is equal to the sum of the squares of the lengths of the legs; that is, $c^2 = a^2 + b^2$.

Converse of the Pythagorean Theorem 5.4.2: If the square of the length of one side of a triangle equals the sum of the squares of the lengths of the other two sides, then the triangle is a right triangle.

Pythagorean Inequalities 5.4.3: For any $\triangle ABC$, with c as the length of its longest side,

If $c^2 = a^2 + b^2$, then $\triangle ABC$ is a right triangle.

If $c^2 > a^2 + b^2$, then $\triangle ABC$ is an obtuse triangle.

If $c^2 < a^2 + b^2$, then $\triangle ABC$ is an acute triangle.

Key Skills

Find the lengths of the sides of a right triangle by using the Pythagorean Theorem.

Find a in the triangle at right.

By the Pythagorean Theorem, $13^2 = a^2 + 12^2$.

Then, $169 = a^2 + 144$, $25 = a^2$, and $a = 5$.

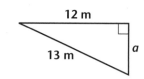

Determine whether a triangle is right, acute, or obtuse by using the Pythagorean inequalities.

Classify the triangle that has sides 14, 20, and 25 as right, acute, or obtuse.

$25^2 = 625$, $20^2 + 14^2 = 596$, and $625 > 596$, so the triangle is obtuse.

Exercises

1. Find c. _____

<table>
<tr><td>16 m</td><td>c</td></tr>
<tr><td></td><td>30 m</td></tr>
</table>

2. Find b. _____

The three side lengths of a triangle are given. Classify the triangle as right, acute, or obtuse.

3. 12, 14, and 16 _____   **4.** 4.5, 6, and 7.5 _____   **5.** 25, 30, and 40 _____

Student Study Guide

5.5 Special Triangles and Areas of Regular Polygons

Objectives

- Identify and use the 45-45-90 Triangle Theorem and the 30-60-90 Triangle Theorem.
- Identify and use the formula for the area of a regular polygon.

Glossary Terms

apothem   30-60-90 triangle   45-45-90 triangle

Theorems, Postulates, and Definitions

45-45-90 Triangle Theorem 5.5.1: In any 45-45-90 triangle, the length of the hypotenuse is $\sqrt{2}$ times the length of a leg.

30-60-90 Triangle Theorem 5.5.2: In any 30-60-90 triangle, the length of the hypotenuse is 2 times the length of the shorter leg, and the length of the longer leg is $\sqrt{3}$ times the length of the shorter leg.

Area of a Regular Polygon 5.5.3: The area, A, of a regular polygon with apothem a and perimeter p is $A = \frac{1}{2}ap$.

Key Skills

Find side lengths of 45-45-90 triangles.

Find the length of the hypotenuse of the 45-45-90 triangle shown. The length of the hypotenuse in a 45-45-90 triangle is $\sqrt{2}$ times the length of a leg, so the length of the hypotenuse is $21\sqrt{2}$.

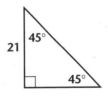

Find side lengths of 30-60-90 triangles.

Find the lengths of the other two sides of the 30-60-90 triangle shown.

The length of the hypotenuse in a 30-60-90 triangle is 2 times the length of the shorter leg, so the length of the shorter leg is $\frac{40}{2} = 20$.

The length of the longer leg of a 30-60-90 triangle is $\sqrt{3}$ times the length of the shorter leg, so the length of the longer leg is $20\sqrt{3}$.

Exercises

1. Find a and b. _____

2. Find a and b. _____

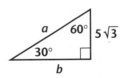

3. Find the area of a regular hexagon with side of length 16 feet and apothem of length $8\sqrt{3}$ feet. _____

Objectives

- Develop and apply the distance formula.
- Use the distance formula to develop techniques for estimating the area under a curve.

Theorems, Postulates, and Definitions

Distance Formula: In a coordinate plane, the distance, d, between two points (x_1, y_1) and (x_2, y_2) is given by the formula:
$d = \sqrt{(x_2 - x_1)^2 + (y_2 - y_1)^2}$.

Key Skills

Determine the distance between two points in a coordinate plane.

Find the distance between the points $(2, 3)$ and $(-6, 9)$.
$d = \sqrt{(-6 - 2)^2 + (9 - 3)^2} = \sqrt{100} = 10$

Estimate the area under a curve by using the method of quadrature.

Use the method of quadrature to estimate the area under the curve $y = \frac{1}{2}x^2$ and above the x-axis from $x = 1$ to $x = 4$.

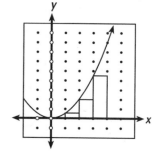

The area can be estimated by three rectangles with a base of 1 and height found by substituting $x = 1$, $x = 2$, and $x = 3$ into $y = \frac{1}{2}x^2$. The heights of the rectangles will be:

$\frac{1}{2}(1^2) = \frac{1}{2}$

$\frac{1}{2}(2^2) = 2$

$\frac{1}{2}(3) = \frac{9}{2}$.

So the estimate of the area is $\frac{1}{2} + 2 + \frac{9}{2} = 7$.

Exercises

Find the distance between each pair of points.

1. $(2, -3)$ and $(-3, 9)$ _____

2. $(-4, 10)$ and $(-11, 34)$ _____

3. Use the method of quadrature to estimate the area under the curve $y = -x^2 + 10$ and above the x-axis from $x = 0$ to $x = 3$. Find the height of each rectangle by substituting the value of the left endpoint of the rectangle into the equation of the curve.

Student Study Guide

5.7 Proofs Using Coordinate Geometry

Objectives

- Develop coordinate proofs for the Triangle Midsegment Theorem, the diagonals of a parallelogram, and the reflection of a point about the line $y = x$.
- Use the concepts of coordinate proofs to solve problems on the coordinate plane.

Key Skills

Prove theorems using coordinate geometry.

Use coordinate geometry to prove that the length of the median to the hypotenuse of a right triangle is equal to half the length of the hypotenuse.

First set up a right triangle on the coordinate plane with vertices at $(0, 0)$, $(2a, 0)$, and $(0, 2b)$ as shown. The midpoint of the

hypotenuse is $\left(\dfrac{2a + 0}{2}, \dfrac{0 + 2b}{2}\right) = (a, b)$.

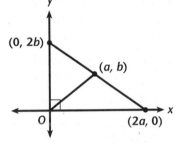

The length of the median to the hypotenuse is

$\sqrt{(a - 0)^2 + (b - 0)^2} = \sqrt{a^2 + b^2}$.

Since (a, b) is the midpoint of the hypotenuse, half the length of the

hypotenuse is $\sqrt{(2a - a)^2 + (0 - b)^2} = \sqrt{a^2 + b^2}$.

Since $\sqrt{a^2 + b^2} = \sqrt{a^2 + b^2}$, the length of the median to the hypotenuse is equal to half the length of the hypotenuse.

Exercises

1. Use coordinate geometry to show that quadrilateral $ABCD$ with vertices $A(0, 0)$, $B(4a, 2b)$, $C(3a, 4b)$, and $D(a, 3b)$ is a trapezoid.

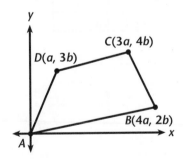

2. Use coordinate geometry and the triangle shown to prove that the medians to the equal sides of an isosceles triangle are equal in length.

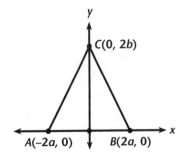

Student Study Guide

5.8 *Geometric Probability*

Objective

- Develop and apply the basic formula for geometric probability.

Glossary Terms

experimental probability   probability   theoretical probability

Key Skills

Find the probability of an event.

What is the probability that a randomly selected point in the rectangle at right is in the shaded triangle?

The area of the rectangle is 600 square meters and the area of the triangle is 250 square meters, so the probability that the point is in the triangle is $\frac{250}{600} = \frac{5}{12} \approx 0.417$.

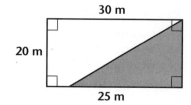

Exercises

In each figure, find the probability that a randomly selected point in the figure is in the shaded area.

1. _____

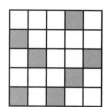

2. ABCD is a trapezoid. _____

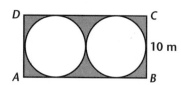

3. _____

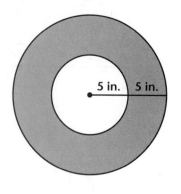

4. *ABCD* is a rectangle. _____

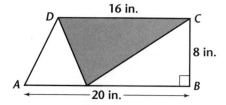

Student Study Guide

6.1 Solid Shapes

Objectives

- Use isometric grid paper to draw three-dimensional shapes built with cubes.
- Develop an understanding of orthographic projection.
- Develop a preliminary understanding of volume and surface area.

Glossary Terms

isometric drawing   orthographic projection

Key Skills

Create isometric drawings of solid figures.

A solid figure is composed of five cubes as shown.
Make an isometric drawing of the solid on grid paper.

Draw orthographic projections of solid figures.

Draw the six orthographic views of the solid shown.

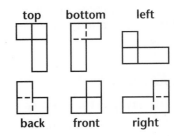

Find volume and surface area of solid figures.

Find the volume and surface area of the solid shown.

The solid is composed of five cubes, so its volume is 5 cubic units. There are 22 exposed cube faces, so its surface area is 22 square units.

Exercises

1. A solid figure is composed of seven cubes as shown. Make an isometric drawing of the solid on grid paper.
2. On a separate sheet of paper, draw the six orthographic views of the solid shown.
3. Find the volume and surface area of the solid shown.

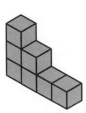

Student Study Guide

6.2 Spatial Relationships

Objectives

- Define *polyhedron*.
- Identify the relationships of points, lines, segments, planes, and angles in three-dimensional space.
- Define *dihedral angle*.

Glossary Terms

dihedral angle	edge	face	half-plane
parallel planes	polyhedron	skew lines	solid
vertex			

Theorems, Postulates, and Definitions

Definition: Polyhedron: A polyhedron is a closed space figure composed of polygons, called the faces of the polyhedron. The intersections of the faces are the edges of the polyhedron. The vertices of the faces are the vertices of the polyhedron.

Definition: Dihedral Angle: A dihedral angle is the figure formed by two half-planes with a common edge. Each half-plane is called a face of the angle, and the common edge of the half-planes is called the edge of the angle.

Key skills

Identify relationships among lines and planes in space.

In the right pentagonal prism shown, name a pair of parallel planes, a pair of perpendicular faces, a pair of skew edges, and an edge and a face that are perpendicular.

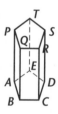

Faces *ABCDE* and *PQRST* are parallel. Faces *ABCDE* and *BCRQ* are perpendicular. $\overline{AB}$ and $\overline{RC}$ are skew edges. $\overline{RC}$ is perpendicular to *ABCDE*.

Exercises

Find the following in the right triangular prism shown.

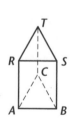

1. Name a pair of parallel faces. _____

2. Name a face that is perpendicular to *RST*. _____

3. Name an edge that is skew to $\overline{AB}$. _____

Student Study Guide

6.3 Prisms

Objectives

- Define *prism, right prism,* and *oblique prism.*
- Examine the shapes of lateral faces of prisms.
- Solve problems using the diagonal measure of a right prism.

Glossary Terms

base   diagonal of a polyhedron   lateral face   oblique prism
prism   right prism

Theorems, Postulates, and Definitions

Diagonal of a Right Rectangular Prism 6.3.1: The length of the diagonal, *d*, of a right rectangular prism is given by $d = \sqrt{\ell^2 + w^2 + h^2}$.

Key Skills

Identify parts of a prism.

In the right prism shown, name the bases, a lateral face, and a lateral edge.
The bases are *ABCD* and *PQRS*. *ABQP* is a lateral face. $\overline{BQ}$ is a lateral edge.

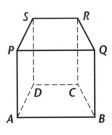

Find the length of a diagonal of a right rectangular prism.

Find the length of a diagonal of a right rectangular prism that has length 10 feet, width 12 feet, and height 15 feet.

$d = \sqrt{10^2 + 12^2 + 15^2} = \sqrt{469} \approx 21.66$ feet.

Exercises

Find the following for the prism shown.

1. Name the bases of the prism. _____

2. Name the lateral faces of the prism. _____

3. Name the lateral edges of the prism. _____

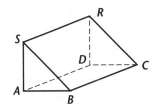

Find the length of a diagonal of a right rectangular prism with the following dimensions.

4. $\ell = 4$ meters; $w = 8$ meters; $h = 12$ meters _____

5. $\ell = 18$ feet; $w = 30$ feet; $h = 40$ feet _____

Objectives

- Identify the features of a three-dimensional coordinate system, including axes, octants, and coordinate planes.
- Solve problems using the distance formula in three dimensions.

Glossary Terms

coordinate plane   first octant   octant   right-handed system
three-dimensional   two-dimensional

Theorems, Postulates, and Definitions

Distance Formula in Three Dimensions 6.4.1: The distance, d, between the points (x_1, y_1, z_1) and (x_2, y_2, z_2) in space is given by
$d = \sqrt{(x_2 - x_1)^2 + (y_2 - y_1)^2 + (z_2 - z_1)^2}$.

Midpoint Formula in Three Dimensions 6.4.2: The midpoint of a segment with endpoints (x_1, y_1, z_1) and (x_2, y_2, z_2) in space is given by
$\left(\dfrac{x_1 + x_2}{2}, \dfrac{y_1 + y_2}{2}, \dfrac{z_1 + z_2}{2} \right)$.

Key skills

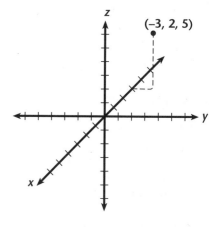

Locate points in a three-dimensional coordinate system.

Locate the point $(-3, 2, 5)$ in a three-dimensional coordinate system.

Find the distance between two points in space.

Find the length of the segment with endpoints $(4, 2, 7)$ and $(7, -3, -4)$.

$d = \sqrt{(7 - 4)^2 + (-3 - 2)^2 + (-4 - 7)} = \sqrt{155} \approx 12.45$

Exercises

Locate each point in a three-dimensional coordinate system. Use a separate sheet of paper.

1. $(3, -2, 4)$ **2.** $(2, 4, -3)$

Find the length of the segment with the given endpoints. Then find the midpoint of the segment.

3. $(6, 7, 4)$ and $(8, 13, 10)$ _____

4. $(-7, -5, 8)$ and $(3, -8, -4)$ _____

Student Study Guide

6.5 Lines and Planes in Space

Objectives

- Define the equation of a line and the equation of a plane in space.
- Solve problems using the equations of lines and planes in space.

Glossary Terms

intercept   parametric equations   trace

Key Skills

Sketch planes in space.

Sketch the plane in space with the equation $3x + 6y + 4z = 12$.

First find the intercepts.
x-intercept: $3x + 6(0) + 4(0) = 12$, so $x = 4$
y-intercept: $3(0) + 6y + 4(0) = 12$, so $y = 2$
z-intercept: $3(0) + 6(0) + 4z = 12$, so $z = 3$

Plot the intercepts and sketch the plane.

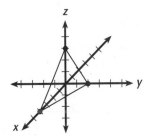

Plot lines in space.

Plot the line in space for these parametric equations.
$x = t + 2$
$y = 3t$
$z = 7t - 2$

When $t = 0$, the point defined by the equations is $(2, 0, -2)$.
When $t = 1$, the point defined by the equations is $(3, 3, 5)$.
Locate these points and sketch the line.

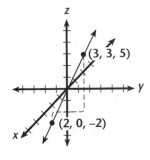

Exercises

1. Sketch the plane in space with the equation $5x - 4y + 10z = 20$.
   Use a separate sheet of paper if necessary.

2. Plot the line in space for the parametric equations. Use a separate
   sheet of paper if necessary.
   $x = 4t$
   $y = 7t - 2$
   $z = 3t + 4$

Student Study Guide
6.6 Perspective Drawing

Objectives

- Identify and define the basic concepts of perspective drawing.
- Apply perspective drawing concepts to creating perspective drawings.

Glossary Terms

one-point perspective   two-point perspective   vanishing point

Theorems, Postulates, and Definitions

Theorem: Sets of Parallel Lines 6.6.1: In a perspective drawing, all lines that are parallel to each other, but not to the picture plane, will seem to meet at a single point known as a vanishing point.

Theorem: Lines Parallel to the Ground 6.6.2: In a perspective drawing, a line that is on the plane of the ground and is not parallel to the picture plane will meet the horizon of the drawing. Any line parallel to this line will meet the horizon at the same point.

Key Skills

Use vanishing points to make perspective drawings.

Make a one-point and a two-point perspective drawing of a rectangular prism.

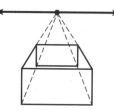

To make a one-point perspective drawing, first draw a rectangle for the front of the prism. Then draw a horizontal line to represent the horizon and mark a vanishing point on the line. From each corner of the rectangle lightly draw lines to your vanishing point. Draw a smaller rectangle whose corners touch the lines to the vanishing point.

To make a two-point perspective drawing, first draw a vertical segment for the front edge of the prism. Draw a horizon line above the segment and place two vanishing points on the line, one on either side of your vertical segment. Draw lines to the vanishing points from the top and bottom of the segment. Draw vertical segments to complete the front of the prism. Draw lines from the endpoints of the segments you just drew to the vanishing points. Use intersection points of the lines to the vanishing points that you just drew as the remaining vertices of the prism.

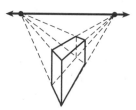

Exercises

For Exercises 1 and 2 use a separate sheet of paper.

1. Make a one-point perspective drawing of a triangular prism using the triangle and vanishing point shown.

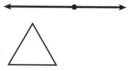

2. Make a two-point perspective drawing of a rectangular prism using the vertical segment and vanishing points shown.

Student Study Guide

7.1 Surface Area and Volume

Objectives

- Explore ratios of surface area to volume.
- Develop the concepts of maximizing volume and minimizing surface area.

Glossary Terms

surface area   volume   surface-area-to-volume ratio

Theorems, Postulates, and Definitions

Surface area and volume of a right rectangular prism 7.1.1: The surface area, S, and volume, V, of a right rectangular prism with length ℓ, width w, and height h are $S = 2\ell w + 2\ell h + 2wh$ and $V = \ell wh$.

Surface area and volume of a cube 7.1.2: The surface area, S, and volume V, of a cube with side s are $S = 6s^2$ and $V = s^3$.

Key Skills

Solve problems using the ratio of surface area to volume.

Determine the surface area to volume ratio for a rectangular prism with $\ell = 5$ meters, $w = 8$ meters, and $h = 10$ meters.

The surface area of a rectangular prism is given by the formula $A = 2\ell w + 2\ell h + 2wh$. So the surface area of this prism is $2(5)(8) + 2(5)(10) + 2(8)(10) = 340$ square meters.

The volume of a rectangular prism is given by the formula $V = \ell wh$. So the volume of this prism is $(5)(8)(10) = 400$ cubic meters.

The ratio of surface area to volume is $\frac{340}{400} = \frac{17}{20} = 0.85$.

Exercises

Find the surface-area-to-volume ratio for each of the following.

1. A rectangular prism with $\ell = 8$ meters, $w = 10$ meters, and $h = 15$ meters. _____

2. A rectangular prism with $\ell = 2$ feet, $w = 10$ feet, and $h = 15$ feet. _____

3. A cube with side of 12 centimeters. _____

4. A cube with a volume of 125 cubic inches. _____

Student Study Guide

7.2 Surface Area and Volume of Prisms

Objectives ～～

- Define and use a formula for finding the surface area of a right prism.
- Define and use a formula for finding the volume of a right prism.
- Use Cavalieri's Principle to develop a formula for the volume of a right or oblique prism.

Glossary Terms ～～

altitude   base   base area   height
lateral area   lateral face

Theorems, Postulates, and Definitions ～～

Surface Area of a Right Prism 7.2.1: The surface area, S, of a right prism with lateral area L, base area B, perimeter p, and height h is $S = L + 2B$ or $S = hp + 2B$.

Cavalieri's Principal 7.2.2: If two solids have equal heights and the cross sections formed by every plane parallel to the bases of both solids have equal areas, then the two solids have equal volume.

Volume of a Prism 7.2.3: The volume, V, of a prism with height h and base area B is $V = Bh$.

Key Skills ～～

Find the surface area of a right prism.

Find the surface area of the right triangular prism shown. The surface area is $S = hp + 2B$. The lateral area is hp or $10(5 + 9 + 11) = 250$ square feet. The area of each base is $\frac{1}{2}(11)(4) = 22$ square feet. So the surface area is $250 + 2(22) = 294$ square feet.

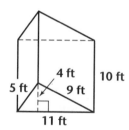

Find the volume of a prism.

Find the volume of the right triangular prism shown.

The volume is $V = Bh$. The area of the base is 22 square feet, so the volume is $(22)(10) = 220$ cubic feet.

Exercises ～～

1. Find the lateral area, the surface area, and the volume of this right triangular prism.

_____

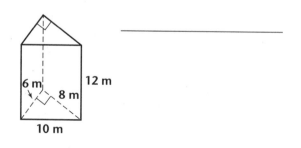

2. Find the lateral area, the surface area, and the volume of this right trapezoidal prism.

_____

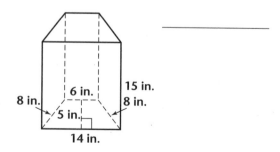

Student Study Guide

7.3 Surface Area and Volume of Pyramids

Objectives

- Define and use a formula for the surface area of a regular pyramid.
- Define and use a formula for the volume of a pyramid.

Glossary Terms

base edge   lateral edge   pyramid   regular pyramid
slant height   vertex of a pyramid

Theorems, Postulates, and Definitions

Surface Area of a Regular Pyramid 7.3.1: The surface area, S, of a regular pyramid with lateral area L, base area B, perimeter of the base p, and slant height ℓ is $S = L + B$ or $S = \frac{1}{2}\ell p + B$.

Volume of a Pyramid 7.3.2: The volume, V, of a pyramid with height h and base area B is $V = \frac{1}{3}Bh$.

Key skills

Find the surface area of a regular pyramid.

Find the surface area of the regular square pyramid shown.

The pyramid has height $h = 12$ feet and slant height $\ell = 15$ feet. The area of the base is $18^2 = 324$ square feet and the perimeter of the base is $4(18) = 72$ feet since the base is a square. The surface area is $S = \frac{1}{2}\ell p + B = \frac{1}{2}(15)(72) + 324 = 864$ square feet.

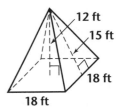

Find the volume of a pyramid.

Find the volume of the pyramid shown.

The volume of a pyramid is $V = \frac{1}{3}Bh = \frac{1}{3}(324)(12) = 1296$ cubic feet.

Exercises

Find the surface area and volume of each regular square pyramid.

1.

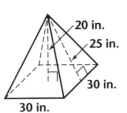

2.

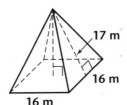

3.

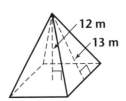

_____

_____

Student Study Guide

7.4 *Surface Area and Volume of Cylinders*

Objectives

- Define and use a formula for the surface area of a right cylinder.
- Define and use a formula for the volume of a cylinder.

Glossary Terms

axis   cylinder   lateral surface   oblique cylinder
right cylinder

Theorems, Postulates, and Definitions

Surface Area of a Right Cylinder 7.4.1: The surface area S of a right cylinder with lateral area L, base area B, radius r, and height h is $S = L + 2B$ or $S = 2\pi rh + 2\pi r^2$.

Volume of a Cylinder 7.4.2: The volume V of a cylinder with radius r, height h, and a base area of B is $V = Bh$ or $V = \pi r^2 h$.

Key Skills

Find the surface area of a right cylinder.

Find the surface area of the right cylinder shown.

The surface area is $S = 2\pi rh + 2\pi r^2 = 2\pi(4)(10) + 2\pi(4^2) = 112\pi \approx$ 351.86 square inches.

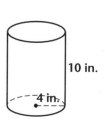

10 in.

4 in.

Find the volume of a cylinder.

Find the volume of the cylinder shown.

The volume is $V = \pi r^2 h = \pi(4^2)(10) = 160\pi \approx 502.65$ cubic inches.

Exercises

Find the surface area and volume of each right cylinder.

1. _____

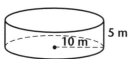

5 m

10 m

2. _____

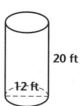

20 ft

12 ft

3. A right cylinder has surface area 320π square centimeters and radius 8 centimeters. Find the height of the right cylinder. _____

Student Study Guide

7.5 Surface Area and Volume of Cones

Objectives

- Define and use the formula for the surface area of a right cone.
- Define and use the formula for the volume of a cone.

Glossary Terms

cone   oblique cone   right cone   vertex of a cone

Theorems, Postulates, and Definitions

Surface Area of a Right Cone 7.5.1: The surface area S of a right cone with lateral area L, base area B, radius r, and slant height ℓ is $S = L + B$ or $S = \pi r \ell + \pi r^2$.

Volume of a Cone 7.5.2: The volume V of a cone with radius r, height h, and base area B is $V = \frac{1}{3}Bh$ or $V = \frac{1}{3}\pi r^2 h$.

Key Skills

Find the surface area of a right cone.

Find the surface area of the right cone shown.

The lateral area is $\pi r \ell = \pi(5)(13) = 65\pi \approx 204.20$ square meters.

The area of the base is $\pi r^2 = 25\pi \approx 78.54$ square meters.

The surface area is $S = L + B = 65\pi + 25\pi = 90\pi \approx 282.74$ square meters.

Find the volume of a cone.

The volume is $V = \frac{1}{3}\pi r^2 h = \frac{1}{3}\pi(5^2)(12) = 100\pi \approx 314.16$ cubic meters.

Exercises

Find the surface area and the volume of each right cone.

1. _____

2. _____

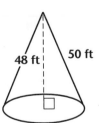

3. Find the surface area of a right cone if it has base area 144π square meters and height 16 meters. _____

4. An oblique cone has volume 3015.93 cubic feet and height 20 feet. Find the radius of the cone. _____

Student Study Guide

7.6 Surface Area and Volume of Spheres

Objectives

- Define and use the formula for the surface area of a sphere.
- Define and use the formula for the volume of a sphere.

Glossary Terms

annulus   sphere

Theorems, Postulates, and Definitions

Volume of a Sphere 7.6.1: The volume V of a sphere with radius r is $V = \frac{4}{3}\pi r^3$.

Surface Area of a Sphere 7.6.2: The surface area S of a sphere with radius r is $S = 4\pi r^2$.

Key Skills

Find the surface area of a sphere.

Find the surface area of a sphere with radius 12 feet.

The surface area is $S = 4\pi r^2 = 4\pi(12)^2 = 576\pi \approx 1809.56$ square feet.

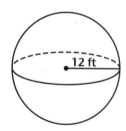

Find the volume of a sphere.

Find the volume of a sphere with radius 12 feet.

The volume is $V = \frac{4}{3}\pi r^3 = \frac{4}{3}\pi(12)^3 = 2304\pi \approx 7238.23$ cubic feet.

Exercises

1. Find the surface area and volume of a sphere with radius 15 meters. _____

2. Find the surface area and volume of a sphere with diameter 36 inches. _____

3. Find the volume of a sphere with surface area 196π square feet. _____

Find the surface area and volume of each figure.

4. _____

5. _____

Student Study Guide

7.7 Three-Dimensional Symmetry

Objectives

- Define various transformations in three-dimensional space.
- Solve problems using transformations in three-dimensional space.

Glossary Terms

solid of revolution

Key Skills

Reflect a figure in a three dimensional coordinate system.

Reflect the segment with endpoints (1, 3, 0) and (2, 6, −1) across the yz plane.

The image has endpoints (−1, 3, 0) and (−2, 6, −1).

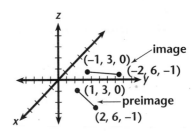

Sketch a solid of revolution.

Sketch the solid of revolution formed by rotating the segment with endpoints (1, 3, 0) and (1, 7, 0) around the y-axis.

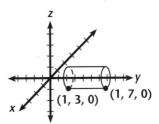

Exercises

1. Reflect the segment with endpoints (2, −4, 3) and (2, −2, 5) across the xz plane.

2. Sketch the solid of revolution formed by rotating the segment with endpoints (0, 0, 3) and (0, 5, 0) around the z-axis.

3. Find the volume of the solid of revolution created in Exercise 2. _____

Student Study Guide

8.1 Dilations and Scale Factors

Objectives

- Construct a dilation of a segment and a point using a scale factor.
- Construct a dilation of a closed plane figure.

Glossary Terms

center of dilation   contraction   dilation
expansion   scale factor

Key Skills

Draw a dilation on a coordinate plane.

Find the image of the segment with endpoints $(-2, 6)$ and $(4, 2)$

after the dilation $D(x, y) = \left(\frac{1}{2}x, \frac{1}{2}y\right)$.

The endpoints of the image are $(-1, 3)$ and $(2, 1)$.

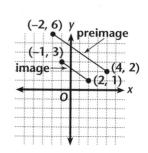

Draw a dilation in a plane.

Dilate the triangle shown about A using the scale factor 3.

Each point on the image is 3 times as far from the center of dilation as the corresponding point on the preimage.

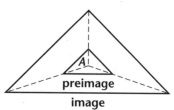

Exercises

1. a. Find the image of the segment with endpoints $(2, -4)$ and $(6, 0)$ transformed by the dilation $D(x, y) = (1.5x, 1.5y)$. Plot the preimage and image on a coordinate plane.

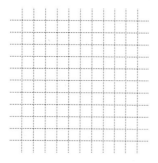

2. Dilate the equilateral triangle shown about A using the scale factor $\frac{1}{3}$.

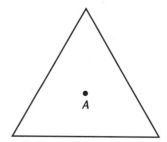

b. Find the slope of the preimage and

image in part **a.** _____

Student Study Guide

8.2 Similar Polygons

Objectives

- Define similar polygons.
- Use properties of proportions and scale factors to solve problems involving similar polygons.

Glossary Terms

proportion   proportional   similar

Theorems, Postulates, and Definitions

Definition: Similar Figures 8.2.1: Two figures are similar if and only if one is congruent to the image of the other by a dilation.

Polygon Similarity Postulate 8.2.2: Two polygons are similar if and only if there is correspondence between their sides and angles so that: 1. All corresponding angles are congruent; 2. All corresponding sides are proportional.

Cross-Multiplication Property 8.2.3: If $\frac{a}{b} = \frac{c}{d}$ and $b, d \neq 0$, then $ad = bc$.

Reciprocal Property 8.2.4: If $\frac{a}{b} = \frac{c}{d}$ and $a, b, c, d \neq 0$, then $\frac{b}{a} = \frac{d}{c}$.

Exchange Property 8.2.5: If $\frac{a}{b} = \frac{c}{d}$ and $b, c, d \neq 0$, then $\frac{a}{c} = \frac{b}{d}$.

"Add-One" Property 8.2.6: If $\frac{a}{b} = \frac{c}{d}$ and $b, d \neq 0$, then $\frac{a+b}{b} = \frac{c+d}{d}$.

Key Skills

Determine whether polygons are similar.

Are the two rectangles shown similar? Explain.
Yes; all angles are 90°, so corresponding angles are

congruent. $\frac{30}{40} = \frac{18}{24} = \frac{3}{4}$, so sides are also proportional.

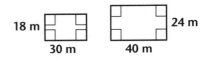

Use proportions to find side lengths of similar figures.

The triangles shown are similar. Find x.

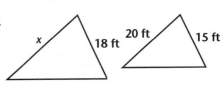

$\frac{15}{18} = \frac{20}{x}$, so $15x = (18)(20) = 360$. Therefore, $x = 24$ feet.

Exercises

Solve each proportion.

1. $\frac{3x}{20} = \frac{5}{2}$ _____

2. $\frac{5x-2}{8} = \frac{4x+5}{4}$ _____

3. Are the parallelograms shown similar? Explain.

4. The triangles shown are similar. Find x.

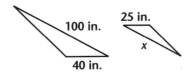

Student Study Guide

8.3 Triangle Similarity Postulates

Objective

- Develop the *AA* Triangle Similarity Postulate and the *SSS* and *SAS* Triangle Similarity Theorems.

Theorems, Postulates, and Definitions

AA (Angle-Angle) Similarity Postulate 8.3.1: If two angles of one triangle are congruent to two angles of another triangle, then the triangles are similar.

SSS (Side-Side-Side) Similarity Theorem 8.3.2: If the three sides of one triangle are proportional to the three sides of another triangle, then the triangles are similar.

SAS (Side-Angle-Side) Similarity Theorem 8.3.3: If two sides of one triangle are proportional to two sides of another triangle and their included angles are congruent, then the triangles are similar.

Key Skills

Use the *AA* Similarity Postulate and the *SSS* and *SAS* Similarity Theorems to determine whether triangles are similar.

Are the triangles shown similar? Name the postulate or theorem that supports your answer.

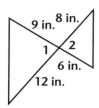

Because they are vertical angles, $\angle 1 \cong \angle 2$. Since $\frac{9}{6} = \frac{12}{8} = \frac{3}{2}$, the two pairs of sides that include those angles are proportional. So the triangles are similar by the *SAS* Similarity Theorem.

Exercises

For each pair of triangles, name the postulate or theorem that proves the triangles similar.

1. _____

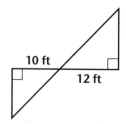

2. _____

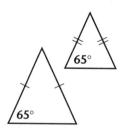

3. _____

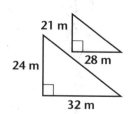

Student Study Guide

8.4 The Side-Splitting Theorem

Objectives

- Develop and prove the Side-Splitting Theorem.
- Use the Side-Splitting Theorem to solve problems.

Theorems, Postulates, and Definitions

Side-Splitting Theorem 8.4.1: A line parallel to one side of a triangle divides the other two sides proportionally.

Two-Transversal Proportionality Corollary 8.4.2: Three or more parallel lines divide two intersecting transversals proportionally.

Key Skills

Use the Side-Splitting Theorem to solve triangle problems.

In the triangle shown $\overline{AB} \parallel \overline{CD}$. Find x.

$\frac{x}{35} = \frac{24}{42} \Rightarrow 42x = (35)(24) \Rightarrow 42x = 840 \Rightarrow x = 20$ feet

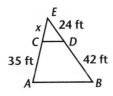

Exercises

Find x in each figure.

1. In the triangle shown $\overline{AB} \parallel \overline{CD}$.

2. In the triangle shown $\overline{AB} \parallel \overline{CD}$.

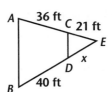

3. In the triangle shown $\overline{AB} \parallel \overline{CD}$.

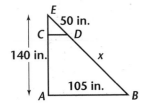
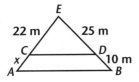

4. In the diagram $\ell \parallel m \parallel n$.

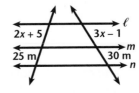

Student Study Guide

8.5 Indirect Measurement and Additional Similarity Theorems

Objectives

- Use triangle similarity to measure distances indirectly.
- Develop and use similarity theorems for altitudes and medians of triangles.

Theorems, Postulates, and Definitions

Proportional Altitudes Theorem 8.5.1: If two triangles are similar, then their corresponding altitudes have the same ratio as their corresponding sides.

Proportional Medians Theorem 8.5.2: If two triangles are similar, then their corresponding medians have the same ratio as their corresponding sides.

Proportional Angle Bisectors Theorem 8.5.3: If two triangles are similar, then their corresponding angle bisectors have the same ratio as their corresponding sides.

Proportional Segments Theorem 8.5.4: An angle bisector of a triangle divides the opposite side into two segments that have the same ratio as the other two sides.

Key Skills

Use similar triangles to measure distance indirectly.

Use the diagram to estimate the width of the lake.

The triangles each contain a right angle and $\angle 1 \cong \angle 2$ because they are vertical angles. So the triangles are similar by the *AA* Similarity Postulate. Let x be the width of the lake.

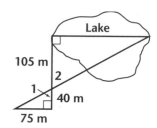

$\frac{x}{75} = \frac{105}{40} \Rightarrow 40x = 7875 \Rightarrow x = 196.875$ meters

Use similarity theorems to solve problems involving altitudes and medians of triangles.

The triangles shown are similar. Find x.

Since the triangles are similar, corresponding medians have the same ratio as the corresponding sides of the triangles.

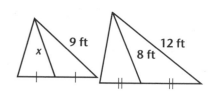

$\frac{12}{9} = \frac{8}{x} \Rightarrow 12x = 72 \Rightarrow x = 6$ feet

Exercises

1. A pole is 20 feet tall and casts a shadow that is 8 feet long. At the same time a building casts a shadow that is 25 feet long. Find the height of the building.

_____

2. The triangles shown are similar. Find x.

_____

3. The triangles shown are similar. Find x.

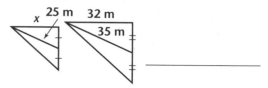

_____

Student Study Guide

8.6 Area and Volume Ratios

Objectives

- Develop and use ratios for areas of similar figures.
- Develop and use ratios for volumes of similar solids.
- Explore relationships between cross-sectional area, weight, and height.

Key Skills

Find the ratios between the areas of similar figures.

The ratio between the sides of two similar triangles is $\frac{3}{5}$. Find the ratio between the areas of the two triangles. The ratio between their areas is $\frac{3^2}{5^2} = \frac{9}{25}$.

Find the ratios between the volumes of similar solids.

The ratio between the radii of two similar cones is $\frac{3}{7}$. Find the ratio between the volumes of the two cones. The ratio between their volumes is $\frac{3^3}{7^3} = \frac{27}{343}$.

Exercises

1. The ratio between the sides of two similar parallelograms is $\frac{4}{5}$. Find the ratio between their areas.

   _____

2. The ratio between the radii of two spheres is $\frac{1}{4}$. Find the ratio between their volumes.

   _____

3. The ratio between the surface areas of two similar pyramids is $\frac{9}{25}$. Find the ratio between their volumes.

   _____

4. The ratio between the volumes of two similar cylinders is $\frac{216}{343}$. Find the ratio between their surface areas.

   _____

5. The height of a cone is 10 inches and the surface area of the cone is 300 square inches. A similar cone has height 12 inches. Find the surface area of the similar cone.

   _____

6. A cylinder has lateral area of 200 square meters and volume of 500 cubic meters. A similar cylinder has surface area 72 square meters. Find the volume of the similar cylinder.

   _____

Student Study Guide

9.1 Chords and Arcs

Objectives

- Define a circle and its associated parts, and use them in constructions.
- Define and use the degree measure of arcs.
- Define and use the length measure of arcs.
- Prove a theorem about chords and their intercepted arcs.

Glossary Terms

arc	arc length	arc measure	center
central angle	chord	circle	diameter
intercepted arc	major arc	minor arc	radius
semicircle			

Theorems, Postulates, and Definitions

Definition: Degree Measure of Arcs 9.1.3: The degree measure of a minor arc is the measure of its central angle. The degree measure of a major arc is 360° minus the degree measure of its central angle. The degree measure of a semicircle is 180°.

Arc Length 9.1.4: If r is the radius of a circle and M is the degree measure of an arc of the circle, then the length, L, of the arc is given by the following: $L = \dfrac{M}{360} (2\pi r)$.

Chords and Arcs Theorem 9.1.5: In a circle, or in congruent circles, the arcs of congruent chords are congruent.

The Converse of the Chords and Arcs Theorem 9.1.6: In a circle, or in congruent circles, the chords of congruent arcs are congruent.

Key Skills

Find central angle measures.

In $\odot M$, find m$\angle AMB$.

Because $180° + 45° + m\angle AMB = 360°$, m$\angle AMB = 135°$.

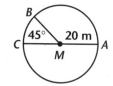

Find arc measures and arc lengths.

In $\odot M$, find m$\overarc{BC}$ and the length of $\overarc{BC}$.

m$\overarc{BC}$ = m$\angle BMC = 45°$, so length of $\overarc{BC} = \dfrac{45°}{360°} (2\pi)(20) = 5\pi \approx 15.71$ meters.

Exercises

Refer to $\odot P$.

1. Name a chord, a diameter, a radius, a central angle, and a major arc with one endpoint at B. _____

2. Find m$\angle BPC$. _____

3. Find m$\overarc{AB}$. _____

4. Find the length of $\overarc{AB}$ to the nearest tenth of a foot. _____

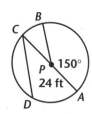

Student Study Guide

9.2 *Tangents to Circles*

Objectives

- Define tangents and secants of circles.
- Understand the relationship between tangents and certain radii of circles.
- Understand the geometry of a radius perpendicular to a chord of a circle.

Glossary Terms

point of tangency   secant   tangent

Theorems, Postulates, and Definitions

Tangent Theorem 9.2.2: If a line is tangent to a circle, then the line is perpendicular to a radius of the circle drawn to the point of tangency.

Radius and Chord Theorem 9.2.3: A radius that is perpendicular to a chord of a circle bisects the chord.

Converse of the Tangent Theorem 9.2.4: If a line is perpendicular to a radius of a circle at its endpoint on the circle, then the line is tangent to the circle.

Theorem 9.2.5: The perpendicular bisector of a chord passes through the center of the circle.

Key Skills

Use properties of secants and tangents to solve problems.

In the figure shown, $\overleftrightarrow{AB}$ is tangent to $\odot P$ at A. $AP = 10$, $PM = 6$, and $PB = 26$. Find AB and CD.

Since $\overleftrightarrow{AB}$ is perpendicular to $\overline{AP}$, $(AP)^2 + (AB)^2 = (PB)^2$.

So, $10^2 + (AB)^2 = 26^2$ and $AB = 24$.

Since $\overline{PE}$ is perpendicular to $\overline{CD}$, $(PM)^2 + (MD)^2 = (PD)^2$.

So, $6^2 + (MD)^2 = 10^2$ and $MD = 8$. Since $\overline{PE}$ bisects $\overline{CD}$, $\overline{CD} = 2(8) = 16$.

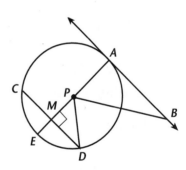

Exercises

In $\odot M$, $CD = 30$, $EM = 8$, and $AB = 20$.
$\overleftrightarrow{AB}$ is tangent to $\odot M$ at A.

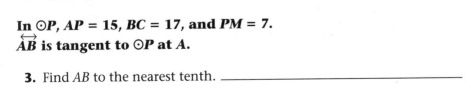

1. Find MA to the nearest tenth. _____

2. Find MB to the nearest tenth. _____

In $\odot P$, $AP = 15$, $BC = 17$, and $PM = 7$.
$\overleftrightarrow{AB}$ is tangent to $\odot P$ at A.

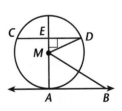

3. Find AB to the nearest tenth. _____

4. Find ED to the nearest tenth. _____

Student Study Guide

9.3 Inscribed Angles and Arcs

Objectives

- Define *inscribed angle* and *intercepted arc*.
- Develop and use the Inscribed Angle Theorem and Corollaries.

Glossary Terms

inscribed angle

Theorems, Postulates, and Definitions

Inscribed Angle Theorem 9.3.1: An angle inscribed in a circle has a measure equal to one-half the measure of the intercepted arc.

Right-Angle Corollary 9.3.2: If an angle is inscribed in a semicircle, then the angle is a right angle.

Arc-Intercept Corollary 9.3.3: If two inscribed angles intercept the same arc, then they have the same measure.

Key Skills

Find the measure of an inscribed angle and its intercepted arc.

Find $m\angle DAB$ and $m\overset{\frown}{BC}$.

Because $\angle DAB$ intercepts a semicircle, $m\angle DAB = 90°$.
Because $m\angle BDC = 20°$, the measure of arc $\overset{\frown}{BC}$ intercepted by $\angle BDC$ is $2(20°) = 40°$.

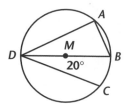

Exercises

$\overline{AC}$ **is a diameter of** $\odot$**M.**

1. Find $m\overset{\frown}{AB}$. _____

2. Find $m\angle ABD$. _____

3. Find $m\overset{\frown}{AD}$. _____

4. Find $m\angle ACD$. _____

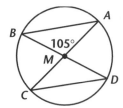

$\overline{AC}$ **is a diameter of** $\odot$**M.**

5. Find $m\angle ABC$. _____

6. Find $m\overset{\frown}{AB}$. _____

7. Find $m\overset{\frown}{BC}$. _____

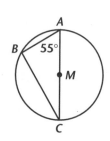

Student Study Guide

9.4 Angles Formed by Secants and Tangents

Objectives

- Define angles formed by secants and tangents of a circle.
- Develop and use theorems about measures of arcs intercepted by these angles.

Theorems, Postulates, and Definitions

Theorem 9.4.1: If a tangent and a secant (or a chord) intersect on a circle at the point of tangency, then the measure of the angle formed is one-half the measure of its intercepted arc.

Theorem 9.4.2: The measure of an angle formed by two secants or chords intersecting in the interior of a circle is one-half the sum of the measures of the arcs intercepted by the angle and its vertical angle.

Theorem 9.4.3: The measure of an angle formed by two secants intersecting in the exterior of a circle is one-half the difference of the measures of the intercepted arcs.

Theorem 9.4.4: The measure of a secant-tangent angle with its vertex outside the circle is one-half the difference of the measures of the intercepted arcs.

Theorem 9.4.5: The measure of a tangent-tangent angle with its vertex outside the circle is one-half the difference of the measures of the intercepted arcs, or the measure of the major arc minus 180°.

Key Skills

Use the angles formed by secants and tangents to solve problems.

In the figure shown, $\overleftrightarrow{AB}$ is tangent to $\odot P$ at A, $m\widehat{AC} = 60°$, $m\widehat{CD} = 70°$, and $m\widehat{DE} = 80°$. Find $m\angle DAB$, $m\angle CBA$, and $m\angle DGC$.

Because the vertex of $\angle DAB$ is on the circle,

$m\angle DAB = \frac{1}{2}\, m\widehat{AD} = \frac{1}{2}\, (60° + 70°) = 65°.$

The vertex of $\angle CBA$ is outside the circle, so $m\angle CBA = \frac{1}{2}\, (m\widehat{EA} - m\widehat{AC}) = \frac{1}{2}\, (150° - 60°) = 45°.$

The vertex of $\angle DGC$ is inside the circle, so $m\angle DGC = \frac{1}{2}\, (m\widehat{EA} + m\widehat{CD}) = \frac{1}{2}\, (150° + 70°) = 110°.$

Exercises

In the figure shown, $\overleftrightarrow{AB}$ is tangent to $\odot P$ at A, $m\widehat{AC} = 135°$, $m\widehat{CD} = 80°$, and $m\widehat{EA} = 90°$. Find the following.

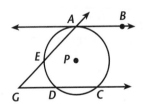

1. $m\angle EGD$ _____

2. $m\angle BAE$ _____

In the figure shown, $m\widehat{AB} = 130°$, $m\widehat{BC} = 30°$, $m\widehat{CD} = m\widehat{DE} = 80°$. Find the following.

3. $m\angle AGE$ _____

4. $m\angle HED$ _____

5. $m\angle BHC$ _____

Student Study Guide

9.5 Segments of Tangents, Secants, and Chords

Objectives

- Define special cases of segments related to circles, including secant-secant, secant-tangent, and chord-chord.
- Develop and use theorems about measures of the segments.

Glossary Terms

external secant segment   secant segment   tangent segment

Theorems, Postulates, and Definitions

Theorem 9.5.1: If two segments are tangent to a circle from the same external point, then the segments are of equal length.

Theorem 9.5.3: If a secant and a tangent intersect outside a circle, then the product of the lengths of the secant segment and its external segment equals the length of the tangent segment squared. (Whole × Outside = Tangent Squared)

Theorem 9.5.2: If two secants intersect outside a circle, then the product of the lengths of one secant segment and its external segment equals the product of the lengths of the other secant segment and its external segment. (Whole × Outside = Whole × Outside)

Theorem 9.5.4: If two chords intersect inside a circle, then the product of the lengths of the segments of one chord equals the product of the lengths of the segments of the other chord.

Key Skills

Use segments formed by tangents, secants, and chords to solve problems.

In the figure shown, $\overleftrightarrow{AB}$ is tangent to $\odot P$ at B, $AH = 9$, $HC = 16$, and $AG = 10$. Find AB and AD.

To find AB use Whole × Outside = Tangent Squared.

$AC \times AH = (25)(9) = (AB)^2$, so $AB = \sqrt{225} = 15$.

To find AD use Whole × Outside = Whole × Outside.
$AC \times AH = AD \times AG = (25)(9) = (AD)(10) \Rightarrow AD = 22.5$

Exercises

In the figure shown, $\overline{AB}$ tangent to $\odot P$ at D, $\overline{BC}$ tangent to $\odot P$ at E, $BD = 20$, $AD = 18$, $AH = 12$, and $GC = 8$. Find the following.

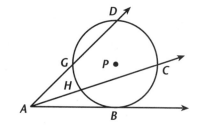

1. BE _____

2. AG _____

3. CE _____

4. In the figure shown, $AG = 15$, $DG = 20$, and $GC = 25$.

Find BG. _____

Student Study Guide

9.6 *Circles in the Coordinate Plane*

Objectives

- Develop and use the equation of a circle.
- Adjust a circle equation to move the center on a coordinate plane.

Key Skills

Sketch a circle from its equation.

Sketch the circle $(x - 2)^2 + (y + 1)^2 = 9$.

The circle has center at $(2, -1)$ and radius 3.

Write the equation of a given circle.

Write an equation of a circle with center $(-4, 6)$ and radius 9.

Using the equation $(x - h)^2 + (y - k)^2 = r^2$ with $h = -4$, $k = 6$, and $r = 9$ yields $(x + 4)^2 + (y - 6)^2 = 81$.

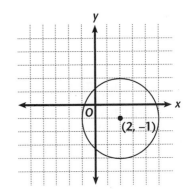

Exercises

1. Write the equation of the circle shown.

_____

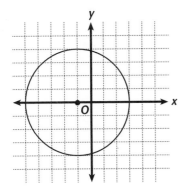

2. Sketch the graph of the circle with equation $(x + 3)^2 + (y - 2)^2 = 25$.

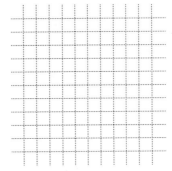

3. Write the equation of the circle with center at $(0, 7)$ and radius 5.

_____

4. Write the equation of the circle with center at $(-4, -3)$ and radius $\sqrt{6.5}$.

_____

5. Find the center and radius of the circle with equation $(x - 2.5)^2 + (y + 6.4)^2 = 70.56$.

_____

6. Write the equation of the circle with center at $(-5, 8)$ that is tangent to the *x*-axis.

_____

7. Write the equation of the circle with center at $(2, 1)$ that contains the point $(8, 9)$.

_____

Student Study Guide

10.1 Tangent Ratios

Objectives

- Develop the tangent ratio using right triangles.
- Use a chart or graph to find the tangent of an angle or the angle for a given tangent.
- Solve problems using tangent ratios.

Glossary Terms

inverse tangent   tangent

Theorems, Postulates, and Definitions

Tangent Ratio 10.1.1: For a given acute angle $\angle A$ with a measure of $\theta°$, the tangent of $\angle A$, or tan θ, is the ratio of the length of the leg opposite $\angle A$ to the length of the leg adjacent to $\angle A$ in any right triangle having A as a vertex, or $\tan \theta = \dfrac{\text{opposite}}{\text{adjacent}}$.

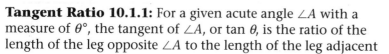

Key Skills

Use right triangles to find tangent ratios.

Find tan θ in the triangle shown.

$$\tan \theta = \frac{\text{opposite}}{\text{adjacent}} = \frac{12}{5}$$

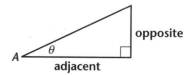

Find an angle that has a given tangent ratio.

Find θ in the triangle shown.

Using a calculator, $\tan^{-1}\left(\dfrac{12}{5}\right) \approx 67.4°$.

Exercises

1. Find tan θ in Figure 1. _____

2. Find θ in Figure 1. _____

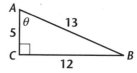

3. Find a in Figure 2. _____

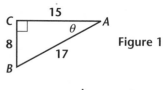

4. Find b and c in Figure 3. _____

_____

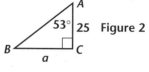

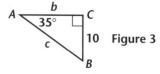

Student Study Guide

10.2 Sines and Cosines

Objectives

- Explore the relationship between the measure of an angle and its sine and cosine.
- Solve problems using sine and cosine ratios.
- Develop two trigonometric identities.

Glossary Terms

cosine   identity   sine

Theorems, Postulates, and Definitions

Sine Ratio 10.2.1: For a given angle $\angle A$ with a measure of $\theta°$, the sine of $\angle A$, or $\sin\theta$, is the ratio of the length of the leg opposite $\angle A$ to the length of the hypotenuse in a right triangle having A as one vertex, or $\sin\theta = \dfrac{\text{opposite}}{\text{hypotenuse}}$.

Cosine Ratio 10.2.2: The cosine of $\angle A$, or $\cos\theta$, is the ratio of the length of the leg adjacent to $\angle A$ to the length of the hypotenuse, or $\cos\theta = \dfrac{\text{adjacent}}{\text{hypotenuse}}$.

Trigonometric Identity 10.2.3: $\tan\theta = \dfrac{\sin\theta}{\cos\theta}$

Trigonometric Identity 10.2.4:
$(\sin\theta)^2 + (\cos\theta)^2 = 1$

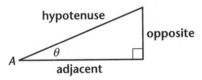

Key Skills

Use right triangles to find sine and cosine ratios.

Find $\sin\theta$ and $\cos\theta$ in the triangle shown.

$\sin\theta = \dfrac{\text{opposite}}{\text{hypotenuse}} = \dfrac{10}{26} = \dfrac{5}{13}$; $\cos\theta = \dfrac{\text{adjacent}}{\text{hypotenuse}} = \dfrac{24}{26} = \dfrac{12}{13}$

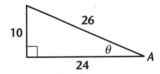

Find an angle that has a given sine or cosine ratio.

Find θ in the triangle shown.

Using a calculator, $\sin^{-1}\left(\dfrac{5}{13}\right) = \cos^{-1}\left(\dfrac{12}{13}\right) \approx 22.62°$.

Exercises

1. Find $\sin\theta$ and $\cos\theta$ in Figure 1.

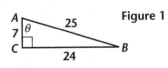

Figure 1

_____

2. Find θ in Figure 1.

3. Find a and b in Figure 2.

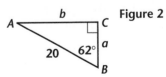

Figure 2

_____

4. Find b and c in Figure 3.

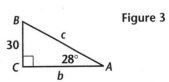

Figure 3

_____

Student Study Guide

10.3 Extending the Trigonometric Ratios

Objectives

- Use a rotating ray on a coordinate plane to define angles measuring more than 90° and less than 0°.
- Define sine, cosine, and tangent for angles of any size.

Glossary Terms

angle of rotation   unit circle

Theorems, Postulates, and Definitions

Unit Circle Definition of Sine and Cosine: Let θ be a rotational angle. Then $\sin\theta$ is the y-coordinate of the image of the point $P(1, 0)$ rotated $\theta°$ about the origin, and $\cos\theta$ is the x-coordinate.

Key Skills

Find the coordinates of a point on the unit circle corresponding to a given angle.

Find the coordinates of point P on the unit circle shown.

Point P has coordinates $(\cos 120°, \sin 120°) \approx (-0.5, 0.8660)$.

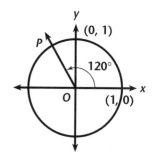

Find the measures of angles given sine or cosine.

Find all angles between 0° and 360° with a sine of 0.8.

Using a calculator, $\sin^{-1} 0.8 \approx 53.13°$ or about 53°. From the graph of $\sin\theta$ we can see there is a second angle with sine of 0.8. The second angle is $180° - 53.13° \approx 126.87$ or about 127°.

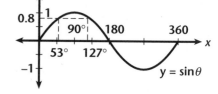

Exercises

1. Find the coordinates of point P on the unit circle shown.

_____

2. Find the coordinates of the image of $P(1, 0)$ after a rotation of $-90°$ about the origin.

_____

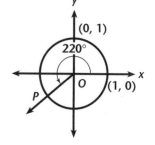

3. Find all angles between 0° and 360° with a sine of 0.6.

_____

Student Study Guide

10.4 The Law of Sines

Objectives

- Develop the Law of Sines.
- Use the Law of Sines to solve triangles.

Theorems, Postulates, and Definitions

The Law of Sines 10.4.1: For any triangle $\triangle ABC$ with sides a, b, and c,

$$\frac{\sin A}{a} = \frac{\sin B}{b} = \frac{\sin C}{c}$$

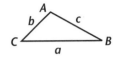

Key Skills

Solve triangles using the Law of Sines.

Use the Law of Sines to solve the triangle shown.

$\frac{\sin 70°}{65} = \frac{\sin B}{49}$, so $\sin B = \frac{49\sin 70°}{65} \approx 0.7084$.

So, $m\angle B = \sin^{-1} 0.7084 \approx 45.1°$.

Then, $m\angle C = 180° - 70° - 45.1° \approx 64.9°$.

Finally, $\frac{\sin 64.9°}{c} = \frac{\sin 70°}{65}$, so $c = \frac{65\sin 64.9°}{\sin 70°} \approx 62.64$.

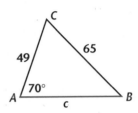

Exercises

1. Solve the triangle in Figure 1.

$\angle A = $ _____

$\angle B = $ _____

$a = $ _____

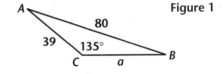

Figure 1

2. Solve the triangle in Figure 2.

$\angle A = $ _____

$a = $ _____

$c = $ _____

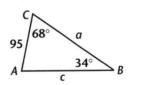

Figure 2

3. Solve the triangle in Figure 3.

$\angle A = $ _____

$\angle B = $ _____

$b = $ _____

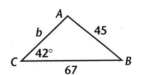

Figure 3

Student Study Guide
10.5 The Law of Cosines

Objectives

- Use the Law of Cosines, together with the Law of Sines, to solve triangles.
- Prove the acute case of the Law of Cosines.

Theorems, Postulates, and Definitions

The Law of Cosines 10.5.1: For any triangle $\triangle ABC$ with sides a, b, and c,

$a^2 = b^2 + c^2 - 2bc \cos A$
$b^2 = a^2 + c^2 - 2ac \cos B$
$c^2 = a^2 + b^2 - 2ab \cos C.$

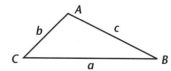

Key Skills

Solve triangles using the Law of Cosines.

Use the Law of Cosines to solve the triangle shown.

Use the first equation of the Law of Cosines to find a.

$a^2 = b^2 + c^2 - 2bc \cos A$
$a^2 = 50^2 + 60^2 - 2(50)(60)\cos 70° \approx 4047.88$
$a = \sqrt{4047.88} \approx 63.62$

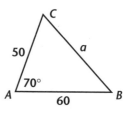

Use the Law of Sines to find $m\angle B$.

$\dfrac{\sin B}{50} = \dfrac{\sin 70°}{63.62} \Rightarrow \sin B = \dfrac{50 \sin 70°}{63.62} \Rightarrow m\angle B \approx 47.6°.$

So $m\angle C = 180° - 70° - 47.6° \approx 62.4°$.

Exercises

1. Solve the triangle in Figure 1.

$\angle A = $ _____

$\angle C = $ _____

$b = $ _____

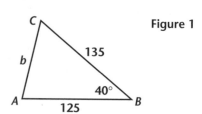

Figure 1

2. Solve the triangle in Figure 2.

$\angle A = $ _____

$\angle B = $ _____

$\angle C = $ _____

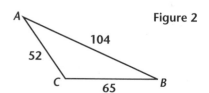

Figure 2

3. Solve the triangle in Figure 3.

$\angle A = $ _____

$\angle B = $ _____

$c = $ _____

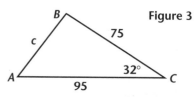

Figure 3

Student Study Guide

10.6 *Vectors in Geometry*

Objectives

- Define vector.
- Add two vectors.
- Use vectors and vector addition to solve problems.

Glossary Terms

direction	displacement vector	head-to-tail method	magnitude
parallelogram method	resultant	vector	vector addition
vector sum			

Key Skills

Find the sum of two vectors using the head-to-tail method and the parallelogram method.

Find the sum of vectors $\vec{a}$ and $\vec{b}$ shown using the head-to-tail method and the parallelogram method.

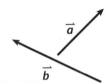

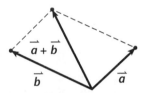

head-to-tail method   parallelogram method

Exercises

1. Find the sum of vectors $\vec{c}$ and $\vec{d}$ using the head-to-tail method or the parallelogram method.

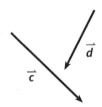

2. In the figure shown, the magnitude of $\vec{a}$ is 50, the magnitude of $\vec{b}$ is 70, and the angle between the two vectors is 100°. Find the magnitude of the resultant vector.

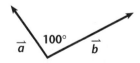

3. Chris walks straight toward the north at 4 miles per hour for 2.5 hours. Chris then turns at a 75° angle and walks straight toward the southwest at 3.5 miles per hour for 2 hours.
   a. At what angle must Chris turn to head directly back to where he started? _____
   b. If he heads directly back, how far will Chris have to walk to get back to where he started? _____

Student Study Guide

10.7 Rotations in the Coordinate Plane

Objectives

- Use transformation equations to rotate points.
- Use a rotation matrix to rotate points or polygons.

Glossary Terms

matrix   rotation matrix   transformation equations

Key Skills

Rotate a point in a coordinate plane by a given angle.

Find the image of the point (5, 3) after a 210° rotation about the origin.

The transformation equations are:

$x' = 5\cos 210° - 3\sin 210° \approx -2.83$ and $y' = 5\sin 210° + 3\cos 210° \approx -5.10$,

so the image of the point is approximately $(-2.83, -5.10)$.

Rotate a polygon in a coordinate plane by a given angle.

Find the image of $\triangle ABC$ with vertices $A(1, 4)$, $B(4, 6)$, and $C(2, 8)$ after a rotation of 270° about the origin.

Multiply the rotation matrix for 270° by the matrix for the triangle.

$$\begin{bmatrix} \cos 270° & -\sin 270° \\ \sin 270° & \cos 270° \end{bmatrix} \begin{bmatrix} 1 & 4 & 2 \\ 4 & 6 & 8 \end{bmatrix} = \begin{bmatrix} 0 & 1 \\ -1 & 0 \end{bmatrix} \begin{bmatrix} 1 & 4 & 2 \\ 4 & 6 & 8 \end{bmatrix} = \begin{bmatrix} 4 & 6 & 8 \\ -1 & -4 & -2 \end{bmatrix}$$

The image $\triangle A'B'C'$ has vertices $A'(4, -1)$, $B'(6, -4)$, and $C'(8, -2)$.

Exercises

1. Find the image of the point (8, 10) after a 135° rotation about the origin.

2. Find the image of the point $(-5, 12)$ after a rotation of $-75°$ about the origin.

3. Find the image of $\triangle ABC$ with vertices $A(0, 5)$, $B(4, 9)$, and $C(3, -6)$ after a rotation of 240° about the origin.

4. Find the image of $\triangle XYZ$ with vertices $X(-2, -6)$, $Y(5, -2)$, and $Z(6, 1)$ after a rotation of 320° about the origin.

Student Study Guide

11.1 *Golden Connections*

Objectives

- Discover the relationship known as the golden ratio.
- Solve problems using the golden ratio.

Glossary Terms

golden ratio   golden rectangle

Key Skills

Determine side lengths of golden rectangles.

A golden rectangle has a long side of length 12 units. Find the length of the short side.

The ratio of the long side to the short side of a golden rectangle is the golden ratio, $\phi \approx 1.618$.

$$\frac{12}{s} = \phi \Rightarrow s = \frac{12}{\phi} \approx 7.417$$

Construct a golden rectangle.

Given square $ABCD$, construct a golden rectangle having short side $\overline{AB}$.
Extend side $\overline{BC}$. Locate M, the midpoint of $\overline{BC}$, and draw an arc centered at M that intersects $\overrightarrow{BC}$ at E. Construct a perpendicular to $\overrightarrow{BC}$ at E and extend $\overline{AD}$ to intersect the perpendicular at F. $ABEF$ is a golden rectangle.

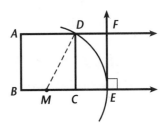

Exercises

Find x in each golden rectangle.

1.

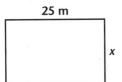

25 m

x

2.

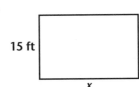

15 ft

x

3. Given square $MNOP$, construct a golden rectangle with short side $\overline{MN}$.

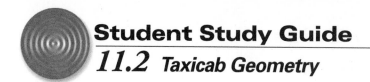

Student Study Guide

11.2 Taxicab Geometry

Objectives ∿∿

- Develop a non-Euclidean geometry based on taxi movements on a street grid known as *taxicab geometry.*
- Solve problems within a taxicab geometry system.

Glossary Terms ∿∿

blocks   taxicab geometry   taxicab circle   taxicab radius
taxidistance

Key Skills ∿∿

Find the taxidistance between two points.

Find the taxidistance between (2, 5) and (7, 3).

The taxidistance between (x_1, y_1) and (x_2, y_2) is $|x_2 - x_1| + |y_2 - y_1|$.
$|7 - 2| + |3 - 5| = 7$

Draw a taxicab circle with a given center and radius.

Draw a taxicab circle centered at (2, 1) with radius 4.

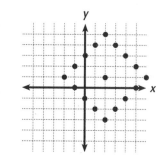

Exercises ∿∿

Find the taxidistance between the following pairs of points.

1. (5, 8) and (2, 4) _____   **2.** (−3, 2) and (9, 7) _____

3. Find the radius of the taxicab circle centered at (−3, −7) that contains the point (−9, 5).

_____

4. Draw the taxicab circle centered at (−1,1) with radius 5.

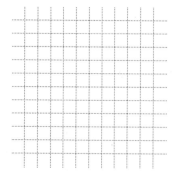

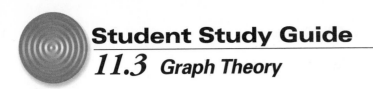

Student Study Guide

11.3 Graph Theory

Objectives

- Determine whether a given graph has an Euler path.
- Use Euler paths to solve problems involving graphs.

Glossary Terms

bridge   degree   edges   Euler circuit
Euler path   even vertex   graph   odd vertex
vertices

Theorems, Postulates, and Definitions

Theorem 11.3.1: A graph contains an Euler path if and only if there are at most two odd vertices.

Key Skills

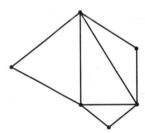

Determine whether a graph contains an Euler path or an Euler circuit.

Does the graph shown contain an Euler path, an Euler circuit, or neither?

The graph contains 6 vertices which are all even. Since there are fewer than two odd vertices, the graph contains an Euler path. Since all the vertices are even, the graph also contains an Euler circuit.

Exercises

Find the following for the graph shown.

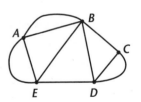

1. Find the degree of vertex *A*.

2. Name all odd vertices.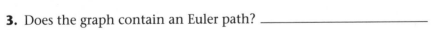

3. Does the graph contain an Euler path?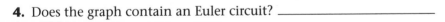

4. Does the graph contain an Euler circuit? _____

Find the following for the graph shown.

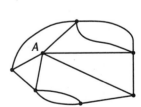

5. Find the degree of vertex *A*. _____

6. How many odd vertices does the graph have? _____

7. Does the graph contain an Euler path? _____

Objectives

- Explore and develop concepts of topology including knots, Möbius strips, and toruses.
- Use theorems of topology to solve problems.

Glossary Terms

Euler characteristic	invariant	Möbius strip
simple closed curve	topology	topologically equivalent
torus		

Theorems, Postulates, and Definitions

Jordan Curve Theorem 11.4.1: Every simple closed curve divides the plane into two distinct regions, the inside and the outside. Every curve that connects a point on the inside to a point on the outside must intersect the curve.

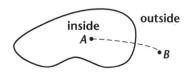

Euler's Formula 11.4.2: For any polyhedron with V vertices, E edges, and F faces, $V - E + F = 2$.

Key Skills

Determine whether two figures are topologically equivalent.

Are the figures shown topologically equivalent?

The figure on the left is a simple closed curve. The figure on the right is not a simple closed curve because it intersects itself. So the figures are not topologically equivalent.

Find topological invariants in a figure.

Find the Euler characteristic of the figure shown.

The figure has 6 vertices, 9 edges, and 5 faces.
The Euler characteristic is $V - E + F = 6 - 9 + 5 = 2$.

Exercises

1. Which of the figures shown are topologically equivalent? Explain.

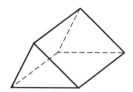

_____

_____

2. Find the Euler characteristic of the figure shown. _____

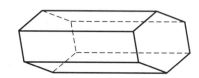

_____

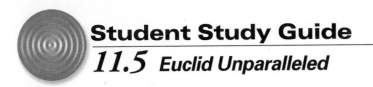
Objectives

- Explore and develop general notions for spherical and hyperbolic geometries.
- Develop informal proofs and solve problems using concepts of non-Euclidean geometries.

Glossary Terms

great circle   hyperbolic geometry   logically equivalent   non-Euclidean
orthogonal   spherical geometry   geometry

Key Skills

Identify lines in spherical geometry.

Name all lines in the model for spherical geometry shown.

In spherical geometry a line is a great circle of the sphere—a circle that divides the sphere into two equal halves. So only $\overleftrightarrow{CD}$ is a line.

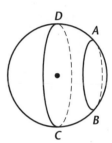

Identify lines in hyperbolic geometry.

Name all lines in the diagram shown for Poincare's model of hyperbolic geometry.

According to Poincare's model, lines are defined as diameters of the outer circle or arcs that are orthogonal to the outer circle. So, $\overleftrightarrow{AB}$ and $\overleftrightarrow{GH}$ are lines.

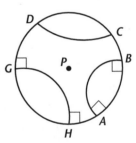

Exercises

1. Name all lines in the spherical geometry model at right.

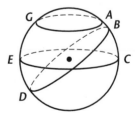

_____

2. Name all lines in the diagram shown for Poincare's model of hyperbolic geometry.

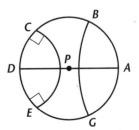

_____

Student Study Guide
11.6 Fractal Geometry

Objectives

- Discover the basic properties of fractals, including self-similarity and iterative processes.
- Build fractal designs using iterative steps.

Glossary Terms

fractal   Cantor Dust   iteration
Menger Sponge   self-similarity   Sierpinski Gasket

Key Skills

Create fractals using iterations.

The fractal is formed by drawing an equilateral triangle on the middle third of each line segment in the figure below and removing the base of the triangle. Draw the first two iterations of the fractal.

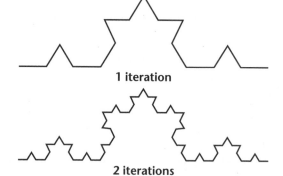

1 iteration

2 iterations

Exercises

The fractal below is formed by dividing a large square into nine smaller squares and removing the four smaller squares that are at the corners of the large square. Repeat the process on all squares remaining in the figure.

1. Draw the first iteration of the fractal.

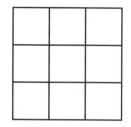

2. Draw the second iteration of the fractal.

Student Study Guide

11.7 Other Transformations: Projective Geometry

Objectives

- Develop the concepts of affine transformations and geometric projection.
- Solve problems and make conjectures using the Theorem of Pappus and the Theorem of Desargues.

Glossary Terms

affine transformation   center of projection   central projection   projective rays

Theorems, Postulates, and Definitions

The Theorem of Pappus 11.7.2: If A_1, B_1, and C_1 are three distinct points on one line and A_2, B_2, and C_2 are three distinct points on a second line, then the intersections of $\overline{A_1B_2}$ and $\overline{A_2B_1}$, $\overline{A_1C_2}$ and $\overline{A_2C_1}$, and $\overline{B_1C_2}$ and $\overline{B_2C_1}$ are collinear.

The Theorem of Desargues 11.7.3: If one triangle is a projection of another triangle, then the intersections of the lines containing the corresponding sides of the two triangles are collinear.

Key Skills

Transform figures using affine transformations.

Draw the preimage and image of the triangle with vertices $(1, 2)$, $(2, -1)$, and $(-3, 0)$ transformed by $T(x, y) = (2x, 3y)$.

$T(1, 2) = (2, 6)$
$T(2, -1) = (4, -3)$
$T(-3, 0) = (-6, 0)$

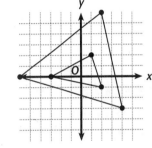

Transform figures using central projections.

Draw a central projection of $\triangle ABC$ centered at point O.

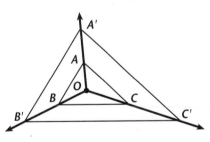

Draw projective rays $\overrightarrow{OA}$, $\overrightarrow{OB}$, and $\overrightarrow{OC}$, and choose points A', B', and C' on the rays. Draw $\triangle A'B'C'$.

Exercises

1. On graph paper draw the preimage and image of the quadrilateral with vertices $(0, 2)$, $(4, 3)$, $(2, -1)$, and $(-2, -3)$ transformed by $T(1.5x, 2y)$.

2. Draw a central projection of $\triangle ABC$ centered at point O.

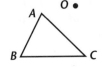

Student Study Guide

12.1 Truth and Validity in Logical Arguments

Objectives

- Define and use the valid argument forms *modus ponens* and *modus tollens*.
- Define and illustrate the invalid forms of *affirming the consequent* and *denying the antecedent*.

Glossary Terms

argument   conclusion   modus ponens   modus tollens
hypothesis   statement   valid argument   valid conclusion

Theorems, Postulates, and Definitions

Argument Form: Modus Ponens 12.1.1:

If *p* then *q*   ←| Hypothesis |
p

Therefore, *q*   ←| Conclusion |

Argument Form: Modus Tollens 12.1.2:

If *p* then *q*   ←| Hypothesis |
Not *q*

Therefore, not *p*   ←| Conclusion |

Invalid Form: Affirming the Consequent 12.1.3:

If *p* then *q*   ←| Hypothesis |
q

Therefore *p*   ←| Conclusion |

Invalid Form: Denying the Antecedent 12.1.4:

If *p* then *q*   ←| Hypothesis |
Not *p*

Therefore, not *q*   ←| Conclusion |

Key Skills

Determine whether an argument is valid or invalid.

Is the following argument valid or invalid?
If it is raining, then the softball team will practice inside.
It is raining.
Therefore, the softball team will practice inside.

The argument is a valid argument of the form *modus ponens*.

Use the Law of Indirect Reasoning

Give a valid conclusion based on the following hypothesis:
If Claire is sick, then she will not go to school.
Claire went to school today.

Using indirect reasoning (*modus tollens*), the statement
Claire is not sick today.
is a valid conclusion.

Exercises

1. Determine whether the following argument is valid or invalid.
   If a batter is hit by a pitch, then the batter goes to first base.
   Chris is on first base.
   Therefore, Chris was hit by a pitch.

2. Use indirect reasoning to give a valid conclusion based on the following hypothesis.
   If a polygon is a convex quadrilateral, then the sum of the measures of its interior angles is 360°.
   The sum of the measures of the interior angles of a polygon is 450°.

Student Study Guide

12.2 And, Or, *and* Not *in Logical Arguments*

Objectives

- Define *conjunction, disjunction,* and *negation.*
- Solve logic problems using conjunction, disjunction, and negation.

Glossary Terms

compound statement	conjunction	disjunction	exclusive *or*
inclusive *or*	negation	truth functionally equivalent	truth table

Key Skills

Write the conjunction and the disjunction of two statements.

Write the conjunction and the disjunction of the following statements:
Geometry is fun.
The World Series is played in October.

Conjunction: *Geometry is fun and the World Series is played in October.*
Disjunction: *Geometry is fun or the World Series is played in October.*

Create a truth table for a compound sentence.

Create a truth table for the disjunction of the statements above.

Let *p* be the statement *"Geometry is fun."* and *q* be the statement *"The World Series is played in October."* Then the truth table for the disjunction *p* OR *q* is the following.

p	*q*	*p* OR *q*
T	T	T
T	F	T
F.	T	T
F	F	F

Exercises

In Exercises 1–4, refer to the following statements:
p: Eating vegetables is healthy.   q: Spring break is too short.

1. Write the conjunction of the given statements. _____

2. Write the disjunction of the given statements. _____

3. Create the truth table for the conjunction of the given statements.

4. Create the truth table for the disjunction of the given statements.

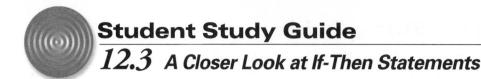

Student Study Guide

12.3 A Closer Look at If-Then Statements

Objectives

- Create truth tables for conditionals and converses, inverses, and contrapositives of conditionals.
- Use if-then statements and forms of valid arguments for problems involving logical reasoning.

Glossary Terms

contrapositive of a conditional   inverse of a conditional

Theorems, Postulates, and Definitions

Summary of the Conditionals: An if-then statement or conditional has three related forms.

Conditional	If p then q	$p \Rightarrow q$
Converse	If q then p	$q \Rightarrow p$
Inverse	If $\sim p$ then $\sim q$	$\sim p \Rightarrow \sim q$
Contrapositive	If $\sim q$ then $\sim p$	$\sim q \Rightarrow \sim p$

Key Skills

Create a truth table for a conditional.

Create a truth table for the following conditional: If it is May, then summer vacation is almost here.

The conditional can be separated into its hypothesis, p, It is May, and its conclusion, q, Summer vacation is almost here. The truth table is the following.

p	q	$p \Rightarrow q$
T	T	T
T	F	F
F	T	T
F	F	T

Write the converse, inverse, and contrapositive of a conditional.

Write the converse, inverse, and contrapositive of the conditional above.

Converse: If summer vacation is almost here, then it is May.
Inverse: If it is not May, then Summer vacation is not almost here.
Contrapositive: If summer vacation is not almost here, then it is not May.

Exercises

Exercises 1–2 refer to the following conditional: If a polygon is a square, then the sum of the measures of its interior angles is 360°.

1. Write the inverse of the given conditional.

_____

2. Create the truth table for the contrapositive of the given conditional.

Student Study Guide

12.4 Indirect Proof

Objectives ～～

- Develop the concept of indirect proof (*reductio ad absurdum* or proof by contradiction).
- Use indirect proof with problems involving logical reasoning.

Glossary Terms ～～

contradiction   indirect proof   proof by contradiction   *reductio ad absurdum*

Theorems, Postulates, and Definitions ～～

Proof by Contradiction 12.4.1: To prove a statement is true, assume it is false and show that this leads to a contradiction.

Key Skills ～～

Use indirect reasoning in proof.

Write an indirect proof.
Given: $\triangle ABC$ with exterior angle $\angle 1$
Prove: $m\angle 1 > m\angle 4$

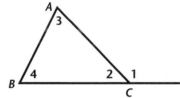

Assume that $m\angle 1 \leq m\angle 4$. By the Exterior Angle Theorem $m\angle 1 = m\angle 4 + m\angle 3$. If $m\angle 1 = m\angle 4$, substitution yields $m\angle 4 = m\angle 4 + m\angle 3$. Then $m\angle 3 = 0°$ which contradicts the fact that the measure of an angle in a triangle is greater than 0°. If $m\angle 1 < m\angle 4$, substitution yields $m\angle 4 + m\angle 3 < m\angle 4$. Then $m\angle 3 < 0°$ which contradicts the fact that the measure of an angle in a triangle is greater than 0°. Since each case leads to a contradiction, this proves indirectly that $m\angle 1 > m\angle 4$.

Exercises ～～

Write an indirect proof.

1. Given: Transversal a intersects lines b and c
   $$m\angle 1 \neq m\angle 3$$
   Prove: Line b is not parallel to line c.

_____

_____

_____

_____

Objectives

- Explore on-off tables, logic gates, and computer logic networks.
- Solve problems by using computer logic.

Glossary Terms

binary number system   input-output table   logic gate

Key Skills

Write a logical expression for a network.

Write a logical expression for the network shown.

(p AND q) OR r

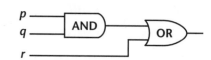

Create input-output tables.

Create an input-output table for the network shown.

p	q	r	p AND q	(p AND q) OR r
1	1	1	1	1
1	1	0	1	1
1	0	1	0	1
1	0	0	0	0
0	1	1	0	1
0	1	0	0	0
0	0	1	0	1
0	0	0	0	0

Exercises

1. Write a logical expression for the network shown.

_____

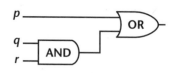

2. Create an input-output table for the network shown.

ANSWERS

Student Study Guide— Chapter 1

Lesson 1.1

1. $\overleftrightarrow{AB}$; $\overrightarrow{AB}$, $\overrightarrow{BA}$, $\overrightarrow{CB}$; $\overline{AB}$, $\overline{AC}$, $\overline{BC}$;
   $\angle BAC$, $\angle ABC$, $\angle ACB$, $\angle 1$, $\angle 2$, $\angle 3$

Lesson 1.2

1. $DF = 10$ 2. $XY = 45$ 3. $MB = 39$

Lesson 1.3

1. $40°; 40°$ 2. $80°$ 3. Yes

Lesson 1.4

1. **a.** Fold point A onto point B.
   b. Fold the line from part **a** onto itself.

2. **a.** Fold $\overrightarrow{BA}$ onto $\overrightarrow{BC}$ such that point B is on the fold.
   b. Fold $\overleftrightarrow{AB}$ onto itself such that point C is on the fold.

Lesson 1.5

1. Sample answer:

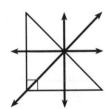

The perpendicular bisectors intersect at the midpoint of the hypotenuse.

2. Sample answer:

3. Sample answer:

Lesson 1.6

1. Sample answer:

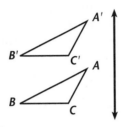

2. Sample answer:

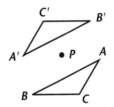

3. Sample answer:

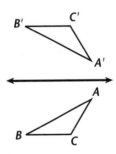

Lesson 1.7

1. $(-5, 0), (-3, -2), (-2, 2)$

2. $(-1, 2), (-3, 0), (-4, 4)$

3. $(-1, -2), (-3, 0), (-4, -4)$

ANSWERS

Student Study Guide — Chapter 2

Lesson 2.1

1. Each term is 4 greater than the previous term.

2. 70; 70; 70; 8(70) = 560

3. The difference between the first term and the second term is the same as the difference between the last term and the second last term. The second term is the same amount bigger than the first term as the second last term is smaller than the last term. So the sum of the first term and the last term is the same as the sum of the second term and the second-to-last term and so on. Since 2 terms are added each time, there will be

   $\frac{n}{2}$ pairs of terms whose sum is the same.

   So the sum of the first n terms will be

   $\frac{n}{2}$ (First term + nth term).

Lesson 2.2

1. Bob received a B on the geometry test.

2. If a person receives a B on a geometry test, then the person scored 87 on the test.; no.

3. A, C, then B

Lesson 2.3

1. c and d

2. A kite is a four-sided figure with two pairs of congruent sides, but opposite sides are not congruent.

3. No. Skew lines also do not intersect. The definition did not restrict the lines to the same plane.

Lesson 2.4

1.

Statements	Reasons
1. $m\angle 2 + m\angle 3 + m\angle 4 = 180°$	1. Given
2. $m\angle 1 + m\angle 2 = 180°$	2. Linear Pair Property
3. $m\angle 1 + m\angle 2 = m\angle 2 + m\angle 3 + m\angle 4$	3. Substitution Property
4. $m\angle 1 = m\angle 3 + m\angle 4$	4. Subtraction Property

Lesson 2.5

1.

Statements	Reasons
1. $m\angle 1 + m\angle 2 = 180°$	1. Given
2. $m\angle 2 = m\angle 3$	2. Vertical Angles Theorem
3. $m\angle 1 + m\angle 3 = 180°$	3. Substitution
4. $m\angle 1 + m\angle 4 = 180°$	4. Linear Pair Property
5. $m\angle 3 = m\angle 4$	5. Congruent Supplements Theorem

Student Study Guide — Chapter 3

Lesson 3.1

1.

The figure has 2-fold rotational symmetry. The image will coincide with the original figure after rotations of 180° and 360°.

2.

The figure has 3-fold rotational symmetry. The image will coincide with the original figure after rotations of 120°, 240°, and 360°.

ANSWERS

Lesson 3.2

1. m∠1 = 135°; m∠2 = 45°

2. *OB* = 10 meters; *CD* = 8 meters

3. m∠*BCD* = 90°; *BD* = 12 inches

4. m∠1 = 90°; m∠*BCD* = 55°

Lesson 3.3

1. **a.** ∠1 and ∠6; ∠5 and ∠6
   b. ∠4 and ∠5

2. m∠3 = 120°; m∠4 = 60°; m∠6 = 120°

3. m∠4 = 38°

Lesson 3.4

1.
Statements	Reasons
1. m∠1 + m∠3 = 180°	1. Given
2. m∠2 + m∠3 = 180°	2. Linear Pair Property
3. m∠1 = m∠2	3. Congruent Supplements Theorem
4. *m* ∥ *n*	4. Converse of the Alternate Interior Angles Theorem

Lesson 3.5

1. m∠1 = 45°   2. m∠1 = 50°

3. m∠1 = 65°; m∠2 = 70°

4. m∠1 = 62°

Lesson 3.6

1. 2880°   2. 165°   3. 30 sides

4. m∠1 = 95°   5. *x* = 130°

Lesson 3.7

1. 23 meters   2. 79 centimeters

3. m∠1 = 63°; *AB* = 44 inches

4. *EF* = 26

Lesson 3.8

1. Perpendicular   2. Parallel

3. (−2, 11)   4. (−12, 6)

Student Study Guide — Chapter 4

Lesson 4.1

1. $\overline{XY}$ 2. $\overline{EA}$ 3. ∠*D*   4. ∠*ZVW*

5. Pentagon *YXWVZ*

6. Answers will vary. Sample: ∠*A* ≅ ∠*T*, $\overline{BC} \cong \overline{UV}$, $\overline{EF} \cong \overline{XY}$

Lesson 4.2

1. △*ADB* ≅ △*CDB* by SAS

2. △*ABC* ≅ △*CDA* by SSS

3. △*ABC* ≅ △*EDC* by ASA

4. △*ACF* ≅ △*DBE* by SAS

Lesson 4.3

1. △*ABE* ≅ △*CBD* by AAS.

2. Triangles are not congruent.

3. Triangles are not congruent.

4. △*ABE* ≅ △*DBC* by HL.

ANSWERS

Lesson 4.4

1.

Statements	Reasons
1. $\overline{AB} \cong \overline{DC}$; $\overline{AF} \cong \overline{DE}$; $n \parallel m$	1. Given
2. $\overline{AE} \cong \overline{DF}$	2. Overlapping Segments Theorem
3. $\angle 1 \cong \angle 2$	3. Alternate Interior Angles Theorem
4. $\triangle ABE \cong \triangle DCF$	4. SAS Theorem
5. $\overline{BE} \cong \overline{CF}$	5. CPCTC

Lesson 4.5

1. That $\overline{AF} \cong \overline{CE}$ is given. Because opposite sides and opposite angles of a parallelogram are congruent, $\overline{AD} \cong \overline{CB}$ and $\angle A \cong \angle C$. $\triangle AFD \cong \triangle CEB$ by SAS.

2. Because $ABCD$ is a rectangle, the diagonals are congruent. Because a rectangle is a parallelogram, the diagonals of $ABCD$ bisect each other. Therefore, $\overline{DE} \cong \overline{CE}$ and $\triangle DCE$ is an isosceles triangle. By the Isosceles Triangle Theorem, $\angle 1 \cong \angle 2$.

Lesson 4.6

1. $ABCD$ is a parallelogram and a rhombus.

2. $ABCD$ is a parallelogram and a rectangle.

3. $ABCD$ is not a parallelogram. (It is an isosceles trapezoid.)

4. $ABCD$ is a parallelogram and a rectangle.

Lesson 4.7

1.

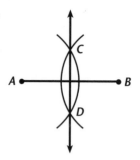

Set your compass equal to a distance greater than half of AB. Place your compass on A and draw an arc. Without adjusting your compass, place the compass point at B. Draw a new arc that intersects the arc you drew from A. Label the intersection points C and D. Use a straightedge to draw $\overleftrightarrow{CD}$. $\overleftrightarrow{CD}$ is the perpendicular bisector of $\overline{AB}$.

2.

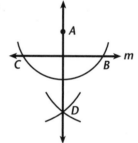

Place your compass point on A and draw an arc through line m. Label the intersection points B and C. Place your compass point at B and draw an arc below the line. Without adjusting your compass, place the compass point at C. Draw an arc that intersects the arc you drew from B and label the intersection point D. Use a straightedge to draw $\overleftrightarrow{AD}$. $\overleftrightarrow{AD}$ is perpendicular to line m.

3.

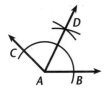

Place your compass at *A* and draw an arc through the rays of the angle. Label the intersection points *B* and *C*. Place your compass point first at *B* and then at *C*. Use the same compass setting to draw arcs that intersect in the interior of ∠*A*. Label the intersection *D*. Draw a ray from *A* through *D*. $\overrightarrow{AD}$ is the bisector of ∠*A*.

4.

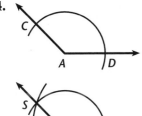

Using a straightedge, draw a ray with endpoint *B*. Place your compass point on *A* and draw an arc through the rays of the angle. Label the intersection points *C* and *D*. Without adjusting your compass, place the compass point at *B*. Draw an arc that crosses the ray and label the intersection point *R*. Set your compass equal to the distance *CD* in ∠*A*. Without adjusting your compass, place the compass point at *R*. Draw an arc that crosses your first arc and label the intersection point *S*. Draw $\overrightarrow{BS}$ to form ∠*B*. ∠*B* is congruent to ∠*A*.

Lesson 4.8

1.

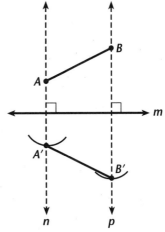

Construct a line, *n*, through *A* perpendicular to line *m* and another line, *p*, through *B* perpendicular to line *m*. Set your compass point on the intersection of lines *m* and *n* and your pencil point at *A*. Draw an arc that crosses line *n*. Label the intersection point *A'*. Set your compass point on the intersection of lines *m* and *p* and your pencil point at *B*. Draw an arc that crosses line *p*. Label the intersection point *B'*. Draw $\overline{A'B'}$. $\overline{A'B'}$ is the reflection of $\overline{AB}$ across line *m*.

2. The third side must be between 8 meters and 32 meters.

Student Study Guide — Chapter 5

Lesson 5.1

1. 100 centimeters

2. Area: 252 square inches; Perimeter: 64 inches

Lesson 5.2

1. △*ABD*: 1500 square meters; *ABCD*: 3000 square meters

2. △*BCD*: 154 square meters; *ABDF*: 192.5 square meters

ANSWERS

Lesson 5.3

1. $C = 30\pi \approx 94.25$ feet;
   $A = 225\pi \approx 706.86$ square feet

2. $C = 26\pi \approx 81.68$ meters;
   $A = 169\pi \approx 530.93$ square meters

3. $A = 36\pi \approx 113.10$ square inches

4. $A = 144 - 36\pi \approx 30.90$ square meters

Lesson 5.4

1. $c = 34$ meters   2. $b = 18$ feet

3. Acute   4. Right   5. Obtuse

Lesson 5.5

1. $a = b = 5\sqrt{2}$

2. $a = 10\sqrt{3}; b = 15$

3. $A = 384\sqrt{3} \approx 665.11$ square feet

Lesson 5.6

1. $d = 13$ 2. $d = 25$ 3. Estimate is 25

Lesson 5.7

1. The slope of $\overline{AB}$ is $\dfrac{2b - 0}{4a - 0} = \dfrac{b}{2a}$.
   The slope of $\overline{CD}$ is $\dfrac{4b - 3b}{3a - a} = \dfrac{b}{2a}$.
   The slope of $\overline{BC}$ is $\dfrac{4b - 2b}{3a - 4a} = -\dfrac{2b}{a}$.
   The slope of $\overline{DA}$ is $\dfrac{3b - 0}{a - 0} = \dfrac{3b}{a}$.
   Since the slopes of $\overline{AB}$ and $\overline{CD}$ are equal, the sides are parallel. Since the slopes of $\overline{BC}$ and $\overline{DA}$ are not equal, the sides are not parallel. Since one pair of sides is parallel and one pair of sides is not parallel, $ABCD$ is a trapezoid.

2. $\overline{AC}$ and $\overline{BC}$ are the equal sides. The
   midpoint of $\overline{AC} = \left(\dfrac{-2a + 0}{2}, \dfrac{0 + 2b}{2}\right) =$
   $(-a, b)$. The midpoint of $\overline{BC} =$
   $\left(\dfrac{2a + 0}{2}, \dfrac{0 + 2b}{2}\right) = (a, b)$.
   The length of the median to $\overline{AC}$ is
   $\sqrt{(2a - (-a))^2 + (0 - b)^2} = \sqrt{9a^2 + b^2}$.
   The length of the median to $\overline{BC}$ is
   $\sqrt{(-2a - a)^2 + (0 - b)^2} = \sqrt{9a^2 + b^2}$.
   Since $\sqrt{9a^2 + b^2} = \sqrt{9a^2 + b^2}$, the lengths of the medians to the equal sides of an isosceles triangle are equal.

Lesson 5.8

1. $\dfrac{7}{25} = 0.28$ 2. $\dfrac{4}{9} \approx 0.444$

3. $\dfrac{1}{4} = 0.25$ 4. $1 - \dfrac{\pi}{4} \approx 0.215$

Student Study Guide — Chapter 6

Lesson 6.1

1.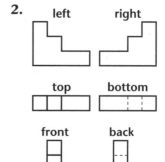

2.

3. Volume: 7 cubic units;
   Surface area: 28 square units

ANSWERS

Lesson 6.2

1. $\triangle ABC$ and $\triangle RST$

2. $ABSR$ or $ACTR$ or $BCTS$

3. $\overline{RT}$ or $\overline{ST}$ or $\overline{TC}$

Lesson 6.3

1. $\triangle ABS$ and $\triangle DCR$

2. $ABCD$, $BCRS$, and $ADRS$

3. $\overline{BC}$, $\overline{SR}$, and $\overline{AD}$

4. $d = \sqrt{224} \approx 14.97$ meters

5. $d = \sqrt{2824} \approx 53.14$ feet

Lesson 6.4

1.

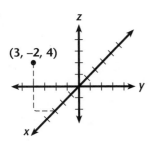

2.

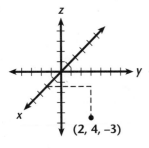

3. $d = \sqrt{76} \approx 8.72$; $(7, 10, 7)$

4. $d = \sqrt{253} \approx 15.91$; $(-2, -6.5, 2)$

Lesson 6.5

1.

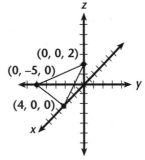

2.

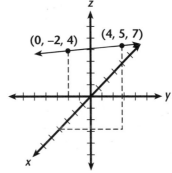

Lesson 6.6

1. Sample answer:

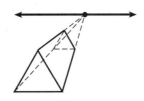

2. Sample answer:

ANSWERS

Student Study Guide — Chapter 7

Lesson 7.1

1. $\frac{7}{12} \approx 0.583$ **2.** $\frac{4}{3} \approx 1.333$

3. $\frac{1}{2} = 0.5$ **4.** $\frac{6}{5} = 1.2$

Lesson 7.2

1. Lateral area: 288 square meters;
Surface area: 336 square meters;
Volume: 288 cubic meters

2. Lateral Area: 540 square inches;
Surface area: 640 square inches;
Volume: 750 cubic inches

Lesson 7.3

1. Surface area: 2400 square inches;
Volume: 6000 cubic inches

2. Surface area: 800 square meters;
Volume: 1280 cubic meters

3. Surface area: 360 square meters;
Volume: 400 cubic meters

Lesson 7.4

1. Surface Area: $300\pi \approx 942.48$ square meters;
Volume: $500\pi \approx 1570.80$ cubic meters

2. Surface area: $312\pi \approx 980.18$ square feet;
Volume: $720\pi \approx 2261.95$ cubic feet

3. $h = 12$ centimeters

Lesson 7.5

1. Surface area: $800\pi \approx 2513.27$ square inches;
Volume: $2560\pi \approx 8042.48$ cubic inches

2. Surface area: $896\pi \approx 2814.87$ square feet;
Volume: $3136\pi \approx 9852.03$ cubic feet

3. $384\pi \approx 1206.37$ square meters

4. $r = 12$ feet

Lesson 7.6

1. Surface area: $900\pi \approx 2827.43$ square meters;
Volume: $4500\pi \approx 14{,}137.17$ cubic meters

2. Surface area: $1296\pi \approx 4071.5$ square inches;
Volume: $7776\pi \approx 24{,}429.02$ cubic inches

3. $\frac{1372\pi}{3} \approx 1436.76$ cubic feet

4. Surface area: $256\pi \approx 804.25$ square feet;
Volume: $\frac{2048\pi}{3} \approx 2144.66$ cubic feet

5. Surface area: $144\pi \approx 452.39$ square cm;
Volume: $288\pi \approx 904.78$ cubic cm

Lesson 7.7

1.

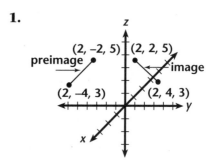

2.

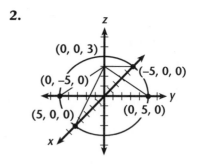

3. $25\pi \approx 78.54$ cubic units

ANSWERS

Student Study Guide — Chapter 8

Lesson 8.1

1. a. The endpoints of the image are $(3, -6)$ and $(9, 0)$.

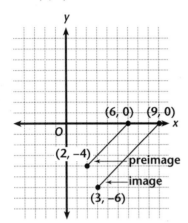

b. Both the preimage and the image have slope of 1.

2.

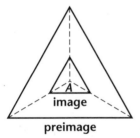

Lesson 8.2

1. $x = \dfrac{100}{6} \approx 16.67$

2. $x = -4$

3. The parallelograms are not similar because $\dfrac{16}{12} \neq \dfrac{10}{8}$.

4. $x = 62.5$ inches

Lesson 8.3

1. *AA* Similarity Postulate

2. *AA* Similarity Postulate or *SAS* Similarity Theorem

3. *SAS* Similarity Theorem or *SSS* Similarity Theorem

Lesson 8.4

1. $x = 8.8$ meters

2. $x = \dfrac{70}{3} \approx 23.33$ feet

3. $x = 150$ inches

4. $x = \dfrac{35}{3} \approx 11.67$ meters

Lesson 8.5

1. The building is 62.5 feet tall.

2. $x = 10$ inches

3. $x = \dfrac{160}{7} \approx 22.86$ meters

Lesson 8.6

1. $\dfrac{16}{25}$ **2.** $\dfrac{1}{64}$ **3.** $\dfrac{27}{125}$ **4.** $\dfrac{36}{49}$

5. 432 square inches

6. 108 cubic meters

Student Study Guide — Chapter 9

Lesson 9.1

1. $\overline{CD}$ or $\overline{AC}$; $\overline{AC}$; $\overline{PA}$, $\overline{PB}$, or $\overline{PC}$; $\angle APB$ or $\angle BPC$; $\overarc{BCA}$

2. m$\angle BPC = 30°$

3. m$\overarc{AB} = 150°$

4. $\overarc{AB} = 20\pi \approx 62.8$ feet

Lesson 9.2

1. $MA = 17$ **2.** $MB \approx 26.2$

3. $AB \approx 28.3$ **4.** $ED \approx 26.5$

ANSWERS

Lesson 9.3

1. $\text{m}\overarc{AB} = 105°$ **2.** $\text{m}\angle ABD = 37.5°$

3. $\text{m}AD = 75°$ **4.** $\text{m}\angle ACD = 37.5°$

5. $\text{m}\angle ABC = 90°$ **6.** $\text{m}\overarc{AB} = 70°$

7. $\text{m}\overarc{BC} = 110°$

Lesson 9.4

1. $\text{m}\angle EGD = 40°$ **2.** $\text{m}\angle BAE = 135°$

3. $\text{m}\angle AGE = 20°$ **4.** $\text{m}\angle HED = 55°$

5. $\text{m}\angle BHC = 35°$

Lesson 9.5

1. $BE = 20$ **2.** $AG = 27$

3. $CE = \sqrt{184} \approx 13.56$ **4.** $BG = 18.75$

Lesson 9.6

1. $(x + 1)^2 + y^2 = 16$

2.

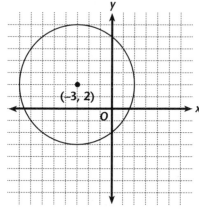

3. $x^2 + (y - 7)^2 = 25$

4. $(x + 4)^2 + (y + 3)^2 = 6.5$

5. Center: $(2.5, -6.4)$; radius = 8.4

6. $(x + 5)^2 + (y - 8)^2 = 25$

7. $(x - 2)^2 + (y - 1)^2 = 100$

Student Study Guide — Chapter 10

Lesson 10.1

1. $\tan \theta = \dfrac{8}{15}$ **2.** $\theta \approx 28.07°$

3. $a \approx 33.18$ **4.** $b \approx 14.28$; $c \approx 17.43$

Lesson 10.2

1. $\sin \theta = \dfrac{24}{25}$; $\cos \theta = \dfrac{7}{25}$ **2.** $\theta \approx 73.74°$

3. $a \approx 9.39$; $b \approx 17.66$ **4.** $b \approx 56.42$; $c \approx 63.90$

Lesson 10.3

1. $P(-0.7660, -0.6428)$ **2.** $P'(0, -1)$

3. $\approx 36.87°$ or $\approx 143.13°$

Lesson 10.4

1. $\text{m}\angle A \approx 24.84°$; $\text{m}\angle B \approx 20.16°$; $a \approx 47.53$

2. $\text{m}\angle A = 78°$; $a \approx 166.18$; $c \approx 157.52$

3. $\text{m}\angle A \approx 85.04°$ or $\text{m}\angle A \approx 94.96°$; $\text{m}\angle B \approx 52.96°$ or $\text{m}\angle B \approx 43.04°$; $b \approx 53.68$ or $b \approx 45.90$

Lesson 10.5

1. $\text{m}\angle A \approx 76.03°$; $\text{m}\angle C \approx 63.97°$; $b \approx 89.42$

2. $\text{m}\angle A \approx 30.75°$; $\text{m}\angle B \approx 24.15°$; $\text{m}\angle C \approx 125.10°$

3. $\text{m}\angle A \approx 51.69°$; $\text{m}\angle B \approx 96.31°$; $c \approx 50.65$

Lesson 10.6

1.

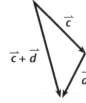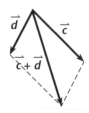

2. 78.64

3. a. 65.45°
   b. 10.62 miles

Lesson 10.7

1. (−12.73, −1.41)

2. (10.30, 7.94)

3. A'(4.33, −2.5); B'(5.79, −7.96);
   C'(−6.70, 0.40)

4. X'(−5.39, −3.31); Y'(2.54, −4.75);
   Z'(5.24, −3.09)

Student Study Guide — Chapter 11

Lesson 11.1

1. $x \approx 15.451$ **2.** $x \approx 24.27$

3.

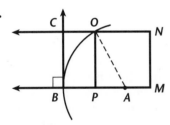

Extend side $\overline{MP}$. Locate A at the midpoint of $\overline{MP}$ and, setting the compass at a radius of $\overline{OA}$, draw an arc centered at A that intersects $\overrightarrow{MP}$ at B. Construct a perpendicular to $\overrightarrow{MP}$ at B and extend $\overline{NO}$ to intersect the perpendicular at C. $MNCB$ is a golden rectangle.

Lesson 11.2

1. 7   **2.** 17   **3.** $r = 18$

4.

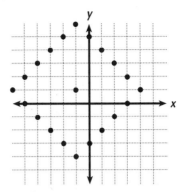

Lesson 11.3

1. 4   **2.** B, C **3.** Yes   **4.** No

5. 5   **6.** 4   **7.** No

Lesson 11.4

1. Figures A and B are both simple closed figures and are topologically equivalent. Because Figure C intersects itself, it is not a simple closed figure and it is not topologically equivalent to figures A and B.

2. 2

Lesson 11.5

1. $\overleftrightarrow{BD}$ and $\overleftrightarrow{CE}$ **2.** $\overleftrightarrow{AD}$ and $\overleftrightarrow{CE}$

Lesson 11.6

1.

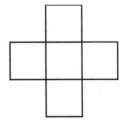

2.

ANSWERS

Lesson 11.7

1.

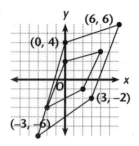

2. Sample answer:

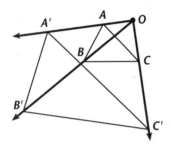

Student Study Guide — Chapter 12

Lesson 12.1

1. The argument is an invalid argument in the form Affirming the Consequent.

2. The polygon is not a convex quadrilateral.

Lesson 12.2

1. *Eating vegetables is healthy and spring break is too short.*

2. *Eating vegetables is healthy or spring break is too short.*

3.

p	q	p AND q
T	T	T
T	F	F
F	T	F
F	F	F

4.

p	q	p OR q
T	T	T
T	F	T
F	T	T
F	F	F

Lesson 12.3

1. If a polygon is not a square, then the sum of the measures of its interior angles is not 360°.

2.

p	q	~p	~q	~q ⇒ ~p
T	T	F	F	T
T	F	F	T	F
F	T	T	F	T
F	F	T	T	T

Lesson 12.4

1. Assume that $b \parallel c$.
Then m∠3 = m∠2 because they are corresponding angles and m∠2 = m∠1 because they are vertical angles. Substitution yields m∠3 = m∠1 which contradicts the given statement that m∠1 ≠ m∠3. This contradiction proves indirectly that line b is not parallel to line c.

Lesson 12.5

1. p OR (q AND r)

2.

p	q	r	q AND r	p OR (q AND r)
1	1	1	1	1
1	1	0	0	1
1	0	1	0	1
1	0	0	0	1
	1	1	1	1
	0	0	0	0
	1	0	0	0
	0	0	0	0